Praise for
Move the World

"Selling something? Persuading someone? Motivating someone? Read *Move the World* and you will. Every time."
—JEFFREY FOX, author of the
New York Times best seller *How to Become CEO*

"With *Move the World*, executives can shorten the time and cost to market by learning to communicate goals and timetables succinctly to their teams, suppliers, investors, advisors, and customers. Mastering Dean's framework is truly essential for entrepreneurial success."
—ELIZABETH RILEY, Adjunct Professor of Entrepreneurship,
Babson College

"The *Move the World* System demystifies the art of persuasion and will give anyone who puts it into use a powerful competitive advantage."
—BRYAN GILDENBERG, Chief Knowledge Officer,
Kantar Retail

"Persuasion *is* vital to success. Dean Brenner recognizes this truth and *Move the World* gives you a clear, powerful system to move your audience and achieve your goals."
—JONATHAN WOLCOTT, Partner, Holland & Knight LLP

"This book is a must-read and an invaluable companion for those who need to communicate effectively with an audience. *Move the World* will help you sell, lead, motivate, and persuade."
—THOMAS D. LIPS, Senior Vice President at
a major international investment firm

"*Move the World* is a great read, and I was able to put the ideas into use immediately. It's the perfect tool for the busy professional who needs to be more persuasive."
—MICHAEL B. DAVIS, Managing Director at
a major international investment bank

Move the World

Move the World

Persuade Your Audience, Change Minds, and Achieve Your Goals

Dean M. Brenner

Persuasion Publishing

Published by Persuasion Publishing.

Library of Congress Cataloging-in-Publication Data:

Brenner, Dean M.
   Move the world : persuade your audience, change minds, and achieve your goals/Dean M. Brenner.
      p. cm.
ISBN: 978-0-692-94379-3 (trade cloth)
1. Business communication.   2. Interpersonal communication.   3. Persuasion (Psychology) I. Title.
   HF5718.B73 2007
   658.4'5—dc22

                                                        2006034742

Printed in the United States of America.

10 9 8 7 6 5 4 3 2 1

*To my wife and dearest friend, Emily,
who once jokingly reminded me that she "grew up in a literate
household," and who starts every day with a smile.
She makes everything possible and everything
worthwhile and is the most beautiful
person I have ever known.*

CONTENTS

An Invitation to Change Your Life, Part I

When you do common things in an uncommon way, you command the attention of the world.

—George Washington Carver

This is a book about something common—communication. It's something we all do, all day, every day. But while this book is about the common act of communication, it is more importantly a book about communicating in an uncommon way. Persuading an audience successfully is not simple, but this book is about simplicity, helping you streamline your preparation so that your professional communication is more effective, powerful, and persuasive.

In *Move the World*, you will discover how people hold ideas and what it takes for them to consider new ones. When you understand what is required to be persuasive, the ways in which you communicate with your colleagues, customers, investors, or stakeholders will change forever.

In an essay for *Power and the Presidency*, edited by Robert Wilson (New York: Public Affairs, 1999), the Pulitzer Prize-winning author and historian David McCullough wrote, "Maybe if we could put presidential power in a pot and boil it all down, a big part of what we would find at the bottom would be language, the use of language, the potency of words. Power to persuade is power indeed, and only a relatively few of the presidents have had it."

Even for those who will never be president, there is power in our words and in the messages we craft. There is no greater or more necessary professional skill than the ability to express yourself verbally and connect with an audience in a memorable way. If you can communicate persuasively, you can add value to any group in any situation.

Who is the *you* I am referring to, and who am I writing for? I am writing for anyone whose success requires the ability to shape or change opinion, influence behavior, or negotiate successfully. You are salespeople; politicians; business leaders, senior executives, and managers; teachers and coaches; fund-raisers, public speakers and presenters; attorneys and consultants—*you* are professionals in all industries. There are many of you.

Do you really need the ability to *move the world* with your words? Does the ability to persuade in a powerful way really affect your daily life? It may seem a lofty goal, unrelated to the reality of your life, because most of us think about our jobs in terms of the next meeting, the next project, or the specific things we need to accomplish today or tomorrow to meet the expectations of those around us. When we commute to the office in the car or on the train, we usually don't think in terms of *moving the world.* We think about the tangible tasks that must be accomplished.

But is having the ability to *move the world* worthwhile? Absolutely. So many of us are consumed by the tasks immediately in front of us that the select few who take the time to develop the critical skills and become persuasive have a significant competitive advantage. The skills in *Move the World* will make you better in everything you do, every day, as you communicate, speak, present, sell, and lead.

Think about your ability to persuade, communicate, sell, or influence. Could you be better—or even significantly better? Let your imagination run a bit. What if every time you had something that you wanted to say, people listened, changed their thinking, and acted on your message? How would that make you feel? Let me ask a slightly different question: Do you remember a moment when you realized you were not being heard, that your words did not matter to your audience? How did that feel?

This book presents a deceptively simple system that will help you communicate more effectively and persuasively every time you speak. Although some of the ideas contained in the system are not new, the system as a whole *is* new. There are two central elements of the *Move the World* System: The first is the Leverage Metaphor; the second is understanding the relationship between your **goals,** your **audience,** and your **plan,** or the GAP Method. The Leverage Metaphor and the GAP Method help in your quest to persuade your audience. Persuasion is not telling people what to think, but shaping what people think about, how they make decisions, and the variables they consider in making their choices. By knowing your *goals,* understanding your *audience*, and following a basic *plan* for a persuasive message, you dramatically increase your ability to be heard.

The individual components of the *Move the World System* are useful on their own, but when the concepts of Leverage and GAP are brought together, they are vastly more powerful. Understanding how a lever works is basic physics. But understanding how to apply it to your communication skills is powerful. Having goals is always a good thing, but without a plan to achieve those goals, the goals don't matter as much. Knowing what you want your audience to think or do when you are done is important, but without the knowledge of the audience's current thinking, it is nearly impossible to create a plan to change their thinking. How can I change the way you think if I don't know what you're thinking to begin with?

When you use the *Move the World* System, you dramatically improve your ability to persuade. You will be able to open locked minds, convince the stubborn, and sell to the people who say, "I'm not buying today." If your goal is to make more money, you will. If your goal is to influence more people, you will.

What *Move the World* Is Not About

- *Move the World* is not about *you*. This book is about your *audience*. When you are in a persuasive situation—a sales call, a speech, a business presentation, or a town meeting—the most important information you must have at your disposal is a deep understanding of your audience. The better you know and understand your audience, the more likely you will be to persuade them of something. In your preparation, your focus should always be the audience. Both the Metaphor and the Method have, at their core, a thorough understanding of your audience.

- *Move the World* is not about *style*. Rather, it is about *substance*. If forced to choose between substance or style as a communicator, choose substance. If you have style as a speaker—a strong voice and the ability to articulate and be entertaining—you have a great skill. But style is no replacement for substance. Without exception, every persuasive, effective communicator has substance. Some also have style. Substance is required, but style on top of substance is a plus. Think about it this way: Great substance delivered without much style *can* still be effective. Great style without much substance *will* ultimately be exposed.

- *Move the World* is not about *developing a new personality*. Successful persuasion requires that you be yourself. I will never ask you to do or be someone you are not. When discussing your delivery skills, I will ask you to pursue one and only one goal: to develop a comfort with your own voice and style. The more authentic you are, the more effective you will be. Authenticity will lead to trust, which will lead to credibility. Authenticity, trust, and credibility are the most important tools at your disposal when presenting your message.

A Warning Label

Please keep in mind that the concepts in this book are powerful, and because of that fact, they must come with a bit of warning. There are several assumptions I make throughout this book:

- I assume that what you are trying to persuade your audience members to do or think will have a positive impact on their lives. I am not interested in arming people with the tools to deceive.

- I also assume that you are good at what you do, and that you are a subject matter expert. This book is not intended to give you a shortcut to success. This book is intended to provide the well-informed, dedicated, honest person with a powerful tool to achieve hard-earned and well-deserved success.

- Persuasion is elusive and difficult. I do not suggest that the *Move the World* System makes persuasion simple. It is not always easy and it is sometimes even impossible to move every audience. Even with this System, it will be a difficult challenge to persuade a Democrat to vote Republican, or vice versa. The System may not be enough to convince a Yankee fan to cheer for the Red Sox. (Believe me, my wife, Emily, has tried.) This book and this System will not always make persuasion automatic, but they provide you with a powerful road map that dramatically increases your chances for success.

Can This Book Change Your Life?

The right book at the right time can change the way we look at ourselves and the world around us. How and why this happens is very personal. What affects me will undoubtedly be different from what affects you, but the common denominator for such books is that they speak to us in ways we can understand. They show us a perspective or a way of thinking that is profound. Perhaps they make life easier for us because we realize that we are not alone and that others face the same challenges we do. Perhaps such books give us a tool, a mind-set, or an attitude that liberates us. Or perhaps they make us more powerful or effective. When a book such as this comes along, it can change your life.

For me, powerful books have changed my life several times. The first time I read *A Catcher in the Rye*, I was 14, and about to begin high school. I was amazed to learn that it was possible that someone else could be as confused about things as I was. Not all that uncommon for a 14 year old, for sure, but in 1983, this was a revelation for me nonetheless. I barely knew who I was or where I wanted to go. As an adult looking back now, I chuckle a bit. It doesn't seem unreasonable to me that a 14 year old does not have his entire life planned out. But when I was there, at that age, in those moments, my lack of direction was not funny to me. *A Catcher in the Rye* let me know that I was not alone.

Shakespeare's *King Lear* was another piece of literature that changed my life. My favorite character, from the very first time I read the play, has always been Lear's faithful servant, Kent. Kent speaks truth to power to the old king, telling him things that no one else can (or will), only to be banished from the kingdom very early in the play. I remember reading Kent's words and realizing that sometimes you have to tell the people you love things they do not want to hear, regardless of the consequences. Kent's honesty is a pure manifestation of his love for his king, which does not end with his banishment. Soon after his banishment, he disguises his appearance and reintroduces himself to his king, continuing to serve Lear. His appearance has changed, but his love and devotion have not. He remains the same faithful friend. Shakespeare, through Kent, teaches us about honesty, tough love, and dedication to the people we care about.

I also remember the first time I read an elegant, though modest, book called *First You Have to Row a Little Boat*. Since the age of 19, I have had a deep love for sailing, and this book captured for me the essence of the sport of sailing as an analogue for life. It liberated me, allowing me to acknowledge that the sport I loved was so much more than just competition. Success on the racecourse requires skills that serve us well in our professions and in life, and this book gave me the license and freedom to connect my sailing to my professional life. This license has had a continued and profound effect on how I think about my business, my clients' businesses, and the many wind shifts that life sends our way. It also was one of the first things that my then not-yet-wife, Emily, and I realized we had in common. We both loved that book—so much so, we chose a passage from it to be read at our wedding several years later.

Finding a common link among Holden Caulfield, Shakespeare's Kent, and an autobiographical story about sailboats is not easy, but it is germane to this discussion. The reason I share them with you is that each has had a profound impact on the way I look at the world. The connection among these three pieces of literature is no more complicated than that. Each shared an idea that taught me something I did not know, liberating me to view my world differently, and subsequently made me more powerful.

Books can and do change our lives. It is my sincere hope that this book will have a profound impact on yours, and that it will help you do the common in an uncommon way.

ACKNOWLEDGMENTS

Many people—too many to mention here—have provided great support and encouragement for this project and for me. But a few deserve some special mention:

- My colleagues at The Latimer Group: Whitney Sweeney, Amy Fenollosa, and Hannah Morris. Each of them is an outstanding colleague. But more importantly, they are all exceptional people. I enjoy seeing them each day.

- The Latimer Group Board of Advisors: Phil Bonanno, Michael Davis, Bryan Gildenberg, Bill Goggins, Alix Hahn, and Josh Levine. This board has been instrumental in bringing The Latimer Group and *Move the World* to life. They have given me their time, expertise, and friendship, for which I am eternally thankful.

- Special mention is appropriate for board member Tom Lips and his wife, Margah. In addition to being loving in-laws, they have always supported Emily and me in everything we have done. They are a great presence in our lives.

- Gerry Sindell, of Thought Leaders International, who took me on as a client and helped give voice to my ideas. Gerry's ability to bring ideas to life is second to none.

ACKNOWLEDGMENTS

- Brett Slater, of Slater's Garage. Brett helps us bring the voice of The Latimer Group to life every day, through our social media, and so much of our content. More importantly, he is a fantastic colleague, who always is willing to do whatever his clients need.

- Mary Ann and Kyle Dostaler of MAD Communications, who have continually helped me evolve and build The Latimer Group. They ask questions, hear my answers, and understand my business. They are great partners of mine.

- Laura Tedeschi, of T2 Creative, who has created the graphics, look, and feel of everything The Latimer Group does. She understands what I am trying to achieve and flawlessly brings it to life—every time.

- Paul Boccardi, a great friend, my college roommate, and a veteran of the publishing world. Paul has always pointed me in the correct direction and offered valuable council with his calm words of wisdom.

- My brother-in-law, Evan, a great writer with a great soul who values the power of friendship. I am excited to see what comes next for you, Evan.

- And finally, many thanks and much love to my family: Keri, Glen, Kristyn, Linda and Tony. Their love and support never waivers, whether I deserve it or not.

Each of these people has contributed to the creation of The Latimer Group and *Move the World* in their own unique and unmistakable way. I am forever grateful.

ABOUT THE AUTHOR

Dean M. Brenner is an experienced executive coach and a recognized expert in teaching persuasive speech. Dean is the founder and president of The Latimer Group, an executive coaching firm focused on helping its clients develop powerful and persuasive communication skills. Dean's client list includes executives and professionals from Fortune 500 and leading organizations in a variety of industries.

In addition to his work with The Latimer Group, Dean served on the Board of Directors of U.S. Sailing for 12 years and served for eight as the Chairman and Team Leader for the U.S. Olympic Sailing Program. Dean led the team at the 2008 and 2012 Olympic Games. Dean is a six-time national sailing champion, was a member of the U.S. Sailing Team for three years and finished second at the 2000 U.S. Olympic Trials.

Dean earned an MBA in finance from the Olin School of Business at Babson College, an MA in Shakespearian literature from the University of Warwick, England, and a BA in English literature and government from Georgetown University. Prior to Georgetown, Dean attended the Kent School in Kent, Connecticut.

Dean and his wife, Emily, live in Wallingford, Connecticut, with their two children and dog.

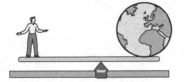

How We Communicate Today—and Why We Are So Bad at It

The mind is a wonderful thing. It starts working the moment you are born and never stops until you get up to speak in public.

—Roscoe Drummond

My professional life is dominated by communication. I study communication and coach it for a living, so I open with a blunt statement—I don't like what I see and hear.

The U.S. economy is no longer primarily industrial, and hasn't been for some time. For most of our history, the U.S. economy has been based on the manufacture of goods. But over the last half of the twentieth century, continued into the twenty-first, there has been a shift in the paradigm. Our economy is now service based—where the real value is found in the exchange of ideas, knowledge, and relationships. The U.S. workforce behind this service-based economy is the hard drive where an organization's core assets—knowledge and relationships—are stored. This reality requires far more skill in how executives and managers communicate with and lead their employees, and in how professionals in all sectors communicate with their customers, investors, colleagues, and stakeholders. No matter how we look at the modern U.S. economy, effective communication is essential for growth and success.

Yet every day of my professional life, I listen to presentations that lack clear points, recommendations, and action steps. I listen to speeches that lack structure and direction. I read and hear sales pitches that neglect to relay the key value of the organization or product or service being sold. I sit in the audience and am usually disappointed by the lack of knowledge the speaker has about me as an individual or about the group as a whole.

3

As consumers, we hear and see advertisements every day that, while humorous, have no true connection to the value proposition of the organization in question. How else can we explain the television fame of a talking gecko? How about beer ad campaigns? The theme of beer ads seems to be this: "If you drink our beer, you'll have the perfect body, six-pack abs, and you'll be surrounded by beautiful specimens of the opposite sex"—and apparently, you'll never stop smiling. But do these ads effectively communicate their message? Consider this: How many times have you watched the ads aired during the Super Bowl, remembered the funny aspect of the ad, but had no recollection of the substance of the ad or even the name of the sponsoring company?

I mention this because modern marketing has a major influence on the way we communicate. Certain successful ad ploys, such as never really discussing the main point of the product, have negatively affected the way we communicate as a culture.

Our culture has come to see verbal subterfuge as an acceptable method of communication. This book stands in opposition to that trend. My contention is that clarity in our communication equals power—the power to influence, affect, and persuade.

Ask Yourself a Few Important Questions

The best way to identify the errors in the way we communicate in the American culture is first to ask yourself a few questions.

How many truly persuasive communicators have you listened to or met during your career? If you are like most people, the answer is few. Why is that? Have you ever listened to a business presentation that seemed to have no structure? I have, too. Most of the presenters I listen to lack structure and direction. How many times has someone walked into a room and completely impressed you with his or her communication skills?

How about a speech or a presentation during which you had no idea what the main point was? I daresay it happens all the time. Have you ever become bored or begun looking at your watch in the first few minutes of a speech? How many times have you felt like the speaker had little understanding of you, your beliefs, or your concerns? At what point in a presentation did smartphones come out? At what point did the audience stop listening?

Why do the phones come out? Perhaps an audience member brings out a phone because he or she is rude or simply too busy to focus. In most cases, the phone comes out because that audience member has lost interest, has moved onto the next thing in his or her life, and feels like his or her time is being wasted. If the presentation or the meeting was truly valuable, even the rude or busy audience member would become engaged and focused and would leave the phone in his or her pocket.

Now let's think about the meetings in your organization. Have you ever been to a meeting that seemingly lasted a lifetime, and at the end, you had little idea what it was all about? How many meetings conclude with no clear understanding of what was just accomplished, or without any idea who was responsible for the next steps? The amount of time we waste in meetings that have no point is nothing less than

5

shocking. Every organization I know, large and small, is guilty of wasting time in meetings.

Here's another example. Let's consider sales calls or sales meetings that you participate in. Have you ever been part of a conversation and were certain the other person wanted you to do something—yet you had no idea what it was? How many times has a salesperson seemed to completely ignore your primary reason for not buying a product or service? Have you ever sat through a sales meeting in which the speaker was not able to change your opinion of his or her organization, product, or service at all?

How about the entrepreneur who presents to potential investors, totally focused on the interesting aspect of his or her product, and totally ignorant of the issues most important to the audience? How about the politician who comes to speak at your chamber of commerce breakfast, and gives you the basic stump speech that has little bearing on the issues affecting you and your neighbors in your district?

The common denominator for all of these issues is that every day in our culture we communicate in poor, ineffective, and incomplete ways. Because of poor communication skills, we leave opportunity on the table. We make it harder on ourselves to lead our organizations, to sell, and to succeed.

We struggle to communicate effectively despite having more information and more communication tools at our disposal than at any other time in human history. In many ways, communication is easy. We have access to data and each other—some would say too much access. We have information, tools, and access.

So what's the problem?

Tools versus Skills

How does the song go? *If I had a hammer, I would hammer in the morning...*

I own a hammer, probably two. I also own a few screwdrivers—some flatheads, some Phillips—a tap and dye set, vise grips, wrenches, a saw, and several cordless tools including a drill and a set of stainless bits.

Any qualified carpenter would feel right at home in my basement. But just because I have the tools does not mean that I am a qualified carpenter. The tools on their own do not magically provide me with the necessary skills to wield them effectively. To become a qualified carpenter, I must work hard to acquire the skills.

This same line of thinking applies to communication. We all own the tools of communication. At the most basic level, we have our voice, a pen, and paper. Thanks to technology, we also have access to the Internet with e-mail in our homes, offices, and, when we travel, on our smartphones and laptops. We have mobile phones and voice mail. In addition, anyone who wants one can get a laptop and give a PowerPoint presentation.

Yes, we all own the tools of communication. And these tools give us access—to each other and to information. We can locate and contact each other with frightening ease. We can receive and dispense information more rapidly and more directly than at any other time in our history.

But simply because we own the tools of communication, are we automatically qualified communicators? Of course not. Yet this conclusion seems to get lost amid our busy lives.

In my work with The Latimer Group, I frequently speak with organizations that justify their purchases of new computers, phone systems, and handheld wireless devices for their employees as an investment in communication. As a result, they assume their staff should automatically be better able to communicate capably and correctly.

Do Any of These Stories Sound Familiar?

Here are a few recent, real-life examples that I have encountered:

- In the first meeting with a new client, a senior executive shared with me a simple but critical issue: "I am concerned that my sales managers and professionals are not communicating well with our clients. I worry they are not telling our story clearly and are not close enough to our clients and prospects. Last year, I spent millions investing in all the electronic communication gadgets they asked me for."

- I recently ran a training class on effective communication for one of our client organizations. The class began with a discussion of what "effective communication" meant to everyone in the room. One woman described herself in the following way: "I am pretty well known in our organization as being a great communicator." I asked her to explain why she had earned that reputation.

  "I keep everyone in the loop," she said. "So, for example, if an important e-mail comes to me I think of everyone who should know about it and I immediately forward it to as many people as possible." But why did this make her a good communicator, I asked. She first responded with a shrug, and then said, "Because that is what communication is. Sharing the information as broadly as possible. Cast a wide net and see what happens."

- One of our clients complained that when her colleagues or manager traveled, they would often answer her e-mail requests with one-word replies or knee-jerk reactions. If there were multiple questions or issues in the e-mail, they often only answered the first question, yet there were many other questions that were raised. Frequently, her questions required more than one-word answers. "It was clear to me they would rapidly fire through their emails, briefly read mine, see the first question, think about it for about 3.2 seconds, and then respond. I know them well enough to know they thought they were being efficient. But if they had just slowed down a bit, they would have been able to give the answer we needed, which in the end would save more time. Instead, their replies caused another full round of e-mails, phone calls, and sometimes meetings."

These classic examples demonstrate some of the most prevalent misconceptions people have about communication. Many organizations and prpfessionals are confused in three important ways:

1. They confuse communication *tools* with communication *skills*.

2. They confuse communication *quantity* with communication *quality*.

3. They confuse communication *speed* with communication *efficiency*.

The array of communication tools that modern technology provides for us creates the illusion that simply enabling communication will automatically improve it, that quantity equals quality, and that speed equals efficiency.

A person's ability to communicate effectively only improves by practicing the necessary skills. Having more tools in your toolbox doesn't necessarily make you a better carpenter, but knowing the right tool to use and using it correctly does.

I coach professionals and executives who have not practiced their presentation or their speech, even though there is great opportunity or risk dependent on their performance. I coach people who do not yet understand their value proposition and have not structured their sales message around it. I see people struggling to tell their story, who do not clearly identify the key points of their presentation, and who make it difficult for their audience to remember and access the information they want and need to convey. I work with intelligent, successful individuals who cannot clearly and persuasively make their point. Because of these underdeveloped skills, their influence is reduced. Deals are not closed. Opportunities are missed.

But it does not have to be this way. The deals can be closed, and the opportunities do not have to be missed—if we change the way we communicate.

What We Do Poorly

Here are the most common and detrimental flaws most individuals in modern U.S. culture make in their communication style:

- *We don't prepare.* We are all busy, struggling to keep up with the work our organizations or colleagues send our way. Many of us spend each day trying to "drink from the fire hose," as the saying goes. Because of this reality, many of the millions of PowerPoint presentations given each day are performed unrehearsed and with little preparation. Because of this reality, most of the millions of sales calls and meetings conducted each day lack proper or sufficient preparation. Because of this reality, we relinquish our power to communicate persuasively.

- *We don't set goals.* We all understand the value of goal setting. We are a goal-oriented society. But it constantly surprises me how many people struggle to answer a question such as, "In your presentation to the board next week, what is your goal? What do you want them to think? What do you want them to do?" Precious few of us set concrete, ambitious, yet realistic, goals for each of our communication opportunities. We set yearly, quarterly, or monthly performance goals, but far fewer of us incorporate our habit of goal-setting into each individual communication opportunity.

- *We don't truly understand our audience.* We live in a culture dominated by airwaves that are filled with people giving us their opinions—cable news, sports talk radio,

11

talk shows, you name it. The programming is filled with people most interested in telling us what they think, and seemingly not at all interested in understanding the issues of their audience. All too often this seems to reinforce the notion that the person who speaks the loudest, speaks last, and does the best job spewing their opinion has won the argument. This cultural reality has infected the way we communicate in general. We have lost sight of the fact that the art of persuasion pivots off an understanding of our audience. How can I persuade you to think differently on a topic if I do not first attempt to understand your current beliefs?

- *We don't make our message memorable or digestible.* With all of the information that comes at us every single day, how can we incorporate all the necessary information and structure our message so that we make it easy for our audience to remember who we are and what we say? On your best day speaking to an interested audience, studies tell us your audience is likely to remember a maximum of 25 percent of what you say 12 hours after your presentation. If you don't identify the most important parts of your message, your audience decides the most memorable aspects of your message. There is no guarantee they will choose what you want them to. Or, worse, they may not remember you at all.

- *We speak too long.* One of my favorite quotations about public speaking comes from the 32nd president, Franklin Delano Roosevelt: "Be clear. Be brief. Be seated." No one has ever uttered the following words after listening to a speech or a presentation: "You know, that was really good and informative. I just wish it was a lot longer." Say what you have to say to make your point and then be done with it. The vast majority of presentations I listen to delve into far too much detail. Most speakers make themselves much harder to listen to because they muddle their key points with far more detail than the audience needs or wants to hear.

The previous list includes many of the most common mistakes I see—and I see all of them all the time. If we recognize these errors, and make some adjustments to the ways we prepare to communicate, these problems can disappear quite easily.

To Inform or to Persuade

There is one more critical but common mistake worth mentioning. Envision for a moment that you are sitting in a meeting within your organization, ready to hear a presentation by one of your colleagues. The presenter starts by saying, "Today I would like to inform you on the progress of our project..."

Or you are in your office and a salesperson who routinely visits you sits down for a meeting and begins by saying, "Thanks for your time today. I would just like to give you a quick update on the performance of our mutual funds. . ." Do these sound familiar? I hear it all the time—in coaching sessions, in training classes, and on the phone with clients. I constantly hear people describe their communications as "updates" or "informational."

Therein lies a critical flaw in the way most of us communicate. At one point or another, most of us segment our professional communication situations—presentations, sales calls, conversations, meetings, speeches, conference calls, or interviews—into two groups. We classify some of our communications as opportunities to persuade. Others, we classify as merely informative.

Segmenting our professional communication scenarios this way is a critical mistake. All your professional communication should be treated as opportunities to *persuade*. None of your professional communication should ever be classified as informative. Why? I will answer that query by way of a story.

Jane, the Project Leader

This is a real example from a client of The Latimer Group, whom I will refer to as "Jane."

Jane works for a manufacturing company and is the project leader on a high-profile, labor-intensive project. To her colleagues and managers, the project appeared to be running behind schedule and exceeding the budget, and they asked Jane to provide a status report. While she felt the project was running as smoothly as could be expected with the limited resources she had been assigned, Jane knew the stakes were high and asked The Latimer Group to help her prepare for her presentation.

We listened to Jane's practice run, and a few questions immediately came to mind:

- *Is Jane trying to inform me or persuade me?* When I pressed her on what her goals were for the presentation, she said "to inform senior management of our progress." That was red flag number one.

- *What does Jane want me to do?* At the end of her presentation, I asked her two questions: "What do you want from me? What do you want me to do?" When she was presented with these simple questions, she said, "Understand where we are on this project." But was that it? Her answers were not articulate or clear. That was red flag number two.

- *What does Jane want me to remember?* I also asked her what she wanted the audience to believe about the project or her team: "When they walk out of the room, what do you want them to remember, above all else?" Again, she had no clear answers. That was red flag number three.

- *Does Jane understand what will concern the audience most?* Jane told us her goal was to prove the project was still worthwhile. But this was a high-profile project, and senior management had already committed to it. Jane did not understand that they were most likely concerned with what she and her team were doing to stay on budget and on schedule. That was red flag number four.

Ultimately, Jane was underestimating her goals and her opportunity for this meeting. To make the project a success, she needed to use the meeting as an opportunity to shape opinion and persuade her audience to think a certain way. She needed to understand what would be most important in the minds of her audience, and also be clear about what she wanted them to know and remember. She needed to persuade senior management to see that the end result remained well within reach, as long as she received additional resources. An update would not be enough. Instead, she needed to attempt to influence the way they viewed the project so that she could get what she needed to be successful.

Lessons from Jane

I see examples like this one from Jane all the time. All of your professional communication should be treated as opportunities to persuade. None of your professional communication should ever be classified as simply informative. When you attempt to merely inform, you are setting yourself up to underachieve in a number of ways. If you know your subject matter, it does not take much preparation to share that information with others. All you have to do is talk. But when you attempt to persuade, to change the way people think, you will quickly realize that more preparation is necessary. Informing is easy. Persuading is not.

If you are Jane's supervisor or manager, you want more value from Jane. You want Jane to do more than stand there and speak. You want Jane to interpret, analyze, and persuade. If Jane communicates in an uncommon way, you, as her manager, will benefit because her out-performance will reflect well on you.

If you are Jane, effective communication will help your career. You will stand out and be in demand. You will be supported and get promoted.

When Jane communicates in an uncommon way, everyone around Jane benefits.

These are the problems on which this book is fundamentally based. The rest of this book is about providing you with strong, yet simple, solutions to these problems and helping you communicate more persuasively and effectively. The *Move the World* System provides you with a powerful way to think about your communication—the Leverage Metaphor—and a powerful way to prepare your message—the GAP Method. Together, they help you bring together many of the simple things that you may have heard before but, most of the time, don't do. The *Move the World* System helps you remember the essence of persuasion and drives you to ask yourself critical questions—the answers to which will make you more powerful.

My goal in this chapter is to engage you with a harsh assessment of the way we communicate as a business culture and encourage you to think more critically about how you communicate. My goal is to begin the process of self-reflection.

Here's one last round of questions for you to consider before we move on to Chapter 2. What about you? Are you confident in your own speaking and communication skills? How persuasive are you? As you are considering your answer to that question, let's begin working on some solutions that will make you significantly more effective.

John Wooden and the UCLA Bruins

I follow sports only to the extent that Tiger Woods only golfs and Jeff Gordon only drives cars—I am a sports fanatic.

The line between sports and entertainment is forever blurred, and I hate it. I hate it when I see a team celebrate a meaningless tackle against a back-up quarterback while losing by three touchdowns in the fourth quarter. Or when I see a basketball player puff out his chest and dance when he dunks on his man, even though his team is losing by 30 points. I suppose getting yourself on Sports Center is more important than actually winning the game.

I began following sports in 1976, when the Yankees made it back to the World Series for the first time since 1964. That was the year I became conscious of the sports world and an active fan. My timing was poor though, and I'm happy to blame my parents. Had I been born earlier, I might have witnessed the tail end of one of the greatest dynasties in sports history.

Over a 12-year period beginning in 1964, John Wooden's UCLA Bruins men's basketball team won 10 national titles in 12 years. And this occurred before the 65-team March Madness tournament field of today. In those days, if you

(continued)

didn't win your conference tournament or title, you didn't qualify for the national tournament. In stark contrast, today we debate whether the sixth *and* the seventh place teams in a major conference will get to play for the national title. Sometimes teams with *losing records* in their conference qualify for the tournament. In Coach Wooden's days, it was a far greater accomplishment to make the national tournament, let alone win it.

Successful teams and organizations are almost always a reflection of their leadership. I have seen video of UCLA games during their glory years. I have watched Kareem Abdul-Jabbar (then known as Lew Alcindor), Bill Walton, and all those great Bruins teams win year after year after year. The most impressive characteristic of Wooden's teams, and the starkest contrast to the world of modern sports, is that his teams never celebrated their many victories in an obnoxious way. He counseled his teams to "never get too high on the highs, and never get too low on the lows." Good advice for all of us, on and off the court. His teams' play and character were defined by integrity.

Wooden preached balance and temperance. His teams reflected his calm leadership and communicated their strength through their actions. When they won, they acted like they deserved to be there (because they did), and like they had been there before (because they had). They were good, worked hard, and celebrated their well-earned success with dignity—just like their leader.

I wish I had been old enough to see those teams in person, but seeing some footage and reading Coach Wooden's philosophies are enough to remind me that without good leadership, most teams are dead on arrival. Teams need many things to succeed, but every successful team absolutely requires someone to set the standard and lead the way.

Coach Wooden set the standard for leadership, not only for his players, but also for everyone who will ever dare call themselves "coach."

For the interested, I highly recommend *They Call Me Coach* by John Wooden.

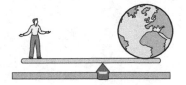

The *Move the World* System: Understanding the Metaphor and the Method

Lots of people act well, but few people speak well. This shows that speaking is the more difficult of the two.

—Oscar Wilde

Recently, I spent several months working with a client who is in sales. Let's call him "John." John and his company had spent resources in the past on sales and presentation training for him and some other members of the sales team. The focus had always been on delivery—eye contact, body language, a good handshake, and the right tone of voice. The focus of all the training had been about the performance aspects of sales.

Taking all of this training to heart, John had even joined the local chapter of an international communication organization to try and learn to speak better "off the cuff." His training had always been all about John—his performance and his delivery. His focus had always been *how* he said things, rather than *what* he said.

As with most people in sales, his goal was simple—sell more. John works hard, understands his product, and is very intelligent and diligent. But he was still not achieving the success he thought he should.

We spent some time together, and he even allowed me to follow him on some sales calls. I sat in his office and listened to him speak with clients and prospects on the phone. I followed him around and listened to him communicate for several days. Before every sales call, we would discuss his plan for achieving success. His answers always centered on his ability to explain why his product was superior. And after every call, we would discuss what occurred, regardless of whether he was successful or not.

His answers to my questions always centered on his own performance. His preparation always focused on himself—*his* message or *his* product. And after the fact, if he was successful, it was due to something *he* had done well. If he was not successful, it was because *he* had failed to execute or had said the wrong thing. The pregame preparation and the postgame analysis always focused entirely on John.

The roadblock for John was clear. He needed to think about his leverage and develop a better understanding of his *goals*, *audience*, and *plan* for success. These elements are the central concepts of this book. With a better understanding of these critical variables, John's ability to sell his product and succeed would improve dramatically.

Understanding the Leverage Metaphor

You have a difficult job ahead of you. There is a heavy object—a 1,000-pound boulder, for example—sitting in front of you, and you need to pick it up. Your success is directly connected to your ability to move this large, seemingly immovable, rock. But you don't see how you will be able to achieve your goal on your own. The object is simply too large and too heavy (see Figure 2.1).

Then you remember a moment from your high school physics class when you learned about the concept of leverage. You remember enough to know that a lever and a fulcrum can be combined to help you. You search and find some suitable items, and your lever seems ready to go.

Figure 2.1   You need help. It's just too heavy.

But high school was a long time ago, and, even then, perhaps you didn't pay close enough attention in physics class. You struggle to lift the boulder, and you try to remember how to use the fulcrum and the lever to help you. Even with these tools at your disposal—which you *know* should help you achieve your goal—you cannot move the boulder. You jump up and down, you push, you wince, yet nothing happens. You simply don't have the strength or the weight to lift it, and you clearly don't know how to use the lever and fulcrum to your maximum advantage (see Figure 2.2).

Now let's adjust the metaphor and replace the object at the other end of the lever with a real-life heavy object each of us encounters every single day. Let's pretend that the seemingly immovable object is your audience in your professional life—your clients, employees, shareholders, boss, voters, jury, students, or congregation. Your goal is to persuade them to think or do something—purchase a product, execute your strategy, invest in your idea, hire you, give

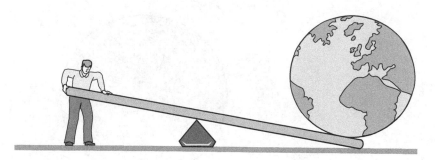

Figure 2.2 How do you use this lever? You know it should help you lift the object, but only when it is used correctly.

you a raise, vote for your candidate, support your platform, deliver the verdict you desire, or learn from your teachings. Your professional success hinges on your ability to change minds, shape opinion, and persuade people to do what you want or need them to do.

Every day of our lives, we all experience many opportunities to change the way people think about us personally and professionally—our project team, product, service, or organization. We are constantly faced with opportunities to persuade an audience to act or think in ways that will help us achieve our goals. Yet here's the reality: Most of us routinely forfeit many of these opportunities by not maximizing the leverage we have available to us. Most of us have a figurative lever and fulcrum available at our disposal, and this lever and fulcrum will dramatically increase our chances for success. Yet most of us do not use the leverage we have to our advantage (see Figure 2.3).

Figure 2.3   You know this is supposed to work. But how?

From Physics Class to Communication

Let's think again about our Metaphor. Take another look at our boulder challenge, and return to our high school physics class. We know that there are three variables available to us that will help us lift our heavy object: The first variable is the position of our fulcrum. Where we place it will have an impact on the power of our lever. The second variable is the length of the lever itself. The longer the lever, the more lifting power we can create. And the third variable is our weight on the end of our lever. The more weight we can apply, the more weight can lift on the other end. Each of these variables can help us if they are positioned in our favor. Conversely, each can hinder us if they are not. And when all three of these variables are in our favor—when the fulcrum is positioned close to the object we want to lift, when our lever is long, and when we can apply sufficient weight on our end of the lever—we can lift almost anything.

Let's think of the first variable, the fulcrum, as our knowledge of our audience. If the audience is the object we want to lift, the better we understand our audience we are speaking to, the closer our fulcrum slides to the object, thereby increasing our leverage. Conversely, the less we know about our audience, the closer our fulcrum slides toward us, reducing our leverage (see Figure 2.4).

The second variable, the lever, is our message, or the words we use to communicate with our audience. The more clearly we have articulated our value, the stronger our message becomes and the longer our lever will be. A good message that clearly articulates a value proposition, anticipates the objections of the audience, and communicates the key

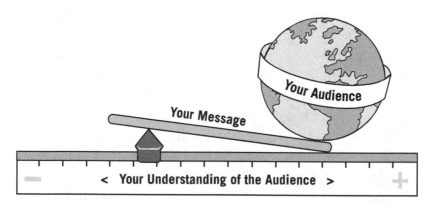

Figure 2.4 Think of your fulcrum as your understanding of your audience. The more you know about them, the closer you move your metaphorical fulcrum toward the object you want to lift.

points is equivalent to a long lever that will increase our leverage. A poorly constructed message that ignores the issues of the audience and does not focus on the important aspects of the proposition is a short lever and gives us no leverage at all (see Figure 2.5).

Finally, let's look at ourselves a little differently as well. We are the third variable. The weight at the left end of the lever is you, me, or anyone who is trying to persuade an audience to do something. Let's think about our own communication skills—our ability to articulate a message, our delivery skills, and our credibility as a person, speaker, or professional. Let's think about these skills as our weight, as the force we can use to lift our object with our lever and fulcrum. The more credibility we have as a speaker, a leader, a salesperson, a lawyer, or a fund-raiser, the more

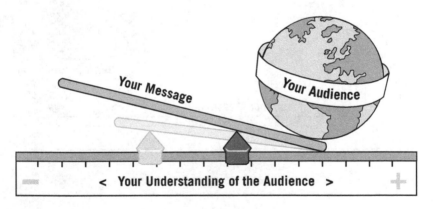

Figure 2.5 Once you understand your audience, and your fulcrum moves in the correct direction, your message (or your metaphorical lever) begins to get longer, giving you a better leverage tool.

figurative weight we can apply to our end of the lever (see Figure 2.6).

Each of the variables in the Leverage Metaphor translates beautifully into a discussion of effective, persuasive communication. If we want to maximize our leverage and lift our boulder, we need a fulcrum placed close to our boulder. We need the longest lever possible and the ability to exert as much force as possible on our end of the lever. If we want to maximize our communication leverage and persuade our audience, we need to place our fulcrum in the correct place, which means we must understand our audience as much as possible. We need a long lever, which means we need a strong, powerful message and communication plan that hits the key points. We need to be able to

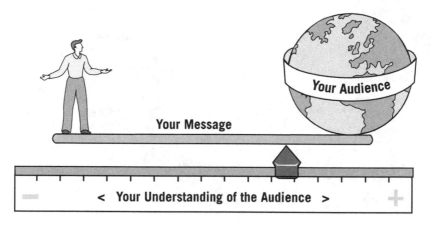

Figure 2.6 Now that your metaphorical fulcrum is moved and your metaphorical lever is lengthened, your credibility, or your potential weight on the lever, increases. And the more credibility we have, the heavier the object we can lift.

exert force and power on our end of the lever, which means we need to be credible and articulate with strong delivery skills. When none of these variables are in our favor, we have no hope of lifting our boulder or persuading our audience. When some, but not all of them, are in our favor we have some hope and some leverage, but not maximum leverage. And when all of them are in our favor, we can lift our boulder, persuade our audience, and move the world.

The Leverage Metaphor fits neatly into a discussion of effective communication, except in one important way: In our boulder example, even if your fulcrum is not in the perfect place, you can still increase your power by finding a longer lever and exerting more weight on your end of the lever. The degree to which each variable is in your favor is not truly dependent on the other variables.

Once we transition into the world of communication, the overall relationship between these three variables changes as well. When we try to persuade our audience rather than lift the boulder, these three variables become much more interdependent. When we try to persuade our audience, everything else becomes much easier if our fulcrum is well placed. Once we understand our audience well, it becomes much easier to have a longer lever and the correct message. And once we understand our audience well and have the correct message, it becomes much easier to establish credibility as a speaker and exert more weight on our end of the lever. Everything flows more easily when we know whom we are speaking to, what their issues and prejudices are, and what they will be most interested in.

All three variables are important—and we want all three to work in our favor, not against us—but our understanding of our audience is the most important. Without a thorough understanding of our audience, our chances for successful persuasion drop dramatically, which leads us to the GAP Method.

Understanding the GAP Method

The primary premise of the GAP Method is simple: Once you truly understand your audience—who they are, what they care about, what their likely objections or concerns will be, or what they are likely to appreciate from your message—it will be far easier for you to craft the appropriate message. The Method gives you a powerful tool to craft and prepare your persuasive message.

To give yourself the greatest chance to persuade your audience, you must have the following three variables in your favor:

1. *Know your goals.* What do you want to achieve in your communication opportunity? What do you want your audience to think about you and your product (organization, client, case, or issue) when you are finished speaking? What do you want your audience to do once they walk out the door? If you don't have clear goals, you forfeit your opportunity to persuade your audience.

2. *Understand your audience.* Who is your audience and where are they coming from? What is your audience's current belief about you and your product (organization, client, case, or issue)? If you don't understand your audience's beliefs, background, or state of mind, you will have a tough time persuading them to think differently.

3. *Map your plan to persuade.* Once you know what your audience thinks today and what you want them to think tomorrow, you must create a logical plan for persuasion and a powerful, compelling message.

As straightforward as the GAP Method may be, knowing how to apply it requires an understanding of the mechanics of communication. When we talk about increasing the power of persuasion, we're really talking about gaining leverage, which becomes easily understood through visualization and a metaphor.

At its core, both the Leverage Metaphor and the GAP Method require an effort to learn as much as possible about the people we are trying to persuade—which brings us back to John.

Lessons from John

John's focus had always been on himself—*his* message, *his* action, *his* performance, and *his* needs. He was almost completely ignoring his audience. He was neglecting to do three things that would have given him leverage:

1. He failed to embrace the notion that his audience is the most important element of the sales leverage equation.

2. Subsequently, he did not attempt to understand his audience as intimately as necessary.

3. Because he did not understand his audience, he was unable to craft a message that communicated with them in a powerful and persuasive way.

Prior to our work together, John had worked solely on his delivery. Delivery is an important variable in your ability to persuade your audience, and if you deliver well you have more metaphorical weight to apply to your end of the lever. However, without a thorough understanding of his audience, and without crafting the appropriate message, John's fulcrum was in the wrong place and his lever was too short. He had only focused on one of the three variables in our Leverage Metaphor—his delivery and his weight on his end of the lever. But without focusing on the other two variables, he would never be able to apply as much weight as he would like and the position of his fulcrum and the length of his lever would work against him.

My work with John consisted of encouraging him to stop worrying about his performance—his eye contact and delivery—and to think about his audience first. I asked him to think about what their perception of him, his company, and his product might be. Why have they not bought from his company in the past? What are their roadblocks? What might cause them to say "yes"?

Once John had a better understanding of his audience, he was able to craft a message that *specifically* addressed their perceptions and the roadblocks to their purchase.

Increasing Your Leverage with the GAP Method

The *Move the World* System works by applying the mechanics of leverage to how we communicate, giving you enormous amounts of potential power. Looking back at our Leverage Metaphor, we increase our leverage and can lift our boulder when the three variables—fulcrum, lever, and weight—are in our favor. We increase our chances for persuasion when we understand our audience, have a plan to deliver the correct message, and when we have credibility and respect as a speaker and as a professional.

Here are four success stories that are examples of how the GAP Method increased the leverage and chance for success in four professional situations: (1) sales, (2) leadership, (3) raising investment capital, and (4) nonprofit fund-raising.

GAP Example 1—Sales

In 2005, a new client came to The Latimer Group with a classic problem. They were not the low-cost producer of their product, yet their customers were increasingly relying on price when making their buying decisions. The choice for this client was clear: reformulate the message and reeducate the customer, or spin into a business death spiral.

I asked the client some questions and learned several important things. Like all customers, theirs would only purchase a product that filled a need. And, like most customers, they would pay a higher price if they perceived greater value. However, we also learned that their customers did not perceive any additional value from my client's product, even though they provided a number of additional services. We needed to communicate the additional benefits and value to take the focus off the price.

At a minimum, the communication challenge in sales is to cause the audience to view the product's value in the appropriate way. Success requires the ability to influence the variables on which the buyer makes their decisions. If a company is not the low-cost producer, they need to make sure price does not drive the purchase decision. If it does, they will lose far more often than they will win.

Only when we truly understand our audience can we make intelligent judgments that lead to the creation of the appropriate message. In this case, the GAP Method led to the creation of a new message that focused repeatedly and aggressively on value and drew value contrasts between my client's product and those of their competitors.

GAP Example 2—Leadership

In 2006, I began working with the owner of a small company. The company had been in business for four years and had weathered difficult times. Revenues were shrinking, and an objective, outside look clearly showed that they were trying to do too many things. Therefore, the owner introduced a new strategy centered on a more focused, streamlined business model. They would offer fewer services and would concentrate their efforts on fewer activities. From an organizational standpoint, this made perfect sense, and the owner was excited to share the plan with his employees.

Almost immediately, however, he received significant resistance from the employees and did not understand why.

When he asked me for help, I read the speech he had given where he announced the new strategy to the employees. On a strategic level, it was a very good speech. He outlined the five major aspects of the plan, and discussed how the organization would benefit. It all made perfect sense—from an organizational standpoint.

But the resistance he had received now made perfect sense to me. His speech lacked much mention of the details the employees would care most about. In this situation, employee audiences are primarily concerned with how the big picture translates and impacts their corner of the world: "How will this affect our project? Our team? Our department? Will people lose their jobs? Will I lose mine?"

When conveying a new direction or strategy, the communication challenge for the business leader consists of making the big picture "real" for the employees. The leader needs to make certain that the conceptual is made tangible.

In this case, we wrote a second speech that filled in many of the blanks, calmed some fears, and eventually the team became aligned around the new strategy.

GAP Example 3—Raising Investment Capital

Several years ago, I spent significant time coaching an entrepreneur. He had led several successful ventures in the past, but his latest had stalled. They needed more capital to stay afloat until revenues improved. Unfortunately, at that time, the market for new investors was even slower than the market for new customers. The entrepreneur had been making the rounds looking for additional capital and had received little interest.

I had him practice his presentation for me, and the problems were immediately clear. The presentation was filled with great examples of the benefits of the company's signature product. But it contained few answers to the questions most investors cared about. Quite simply, the investor always is concerned with three questions: (1) What is my likely return? (2) What is the time frame for seeing that return? (3) What is the exit strategy if things do not go according to plan? All other information needs to be given in the context of answering those three questions.

The communication challenge for the individual raising capital is to spend as little time as possible discussing product features, and as much time as possible quantifying the investment opportunity. Often, the things most important to the entrepreneur are the things least important to the investor.

We redesigned the presentation, answered the three questions, and found plenty of renewed interest.

GAP Example 4—Nonprofit Fund-Raising

From 2005 to 2012, I helped a number of aspiring Olympic sailors with their fund-raising efforts. Some of these athletes competed in the 2004 Olympics and then continued on to 2008 and 2012. One of the athletes shared a frustration with me. She was struggling to describe what the return would be for a donor or a corporate sponsor. This young sailor was focused on trying to deliver a tangible and quantifiable financial return to her donors and sponsors. (The entrepreneur from the previous example should take note.) I understood the frustration, but knew it was destined to continue, unless she changed her approach and her expectations.

The donor in a nonprofit environment cares about helping the cause and wants an emotional connection: "Am I funding a cure? A scholarship? A dream?" They are also concerned with how the dollars they contribute will be spent: "What percentage of my dollar is used to help the cause? What percentage is spent on overhead and other expenses?"

The communication challenge for the nonprofit fund-raiser is clear. It consists of explaining exactly how the contributed dollar will be used and making an emotional connection between the donor and the recipient of the donation.

I worked with this athlete to redesign her message to highlight the need that was being filled, and how the contribution would help her reach her goal. We quantified her training, personal sacrifice, and described her journey. We tried to let the donors live the experience with her. The results were remarkable.

The salesperson, the business leader, the entrepreneur, and the fund-raiser all have a common goal—to persuade their audience to be supportive. The sales audience cares about value. The employee audience cares about how decisions will affect them. The investor audience cares about return. And the nonprofit donor cares about the need they will fill and how the dollars will be spent. In all these situations, any chance for success begins with an understanding of the audience, and then designing the correct message. In all these situations, the GAP Method is a good starting point for creating the plan for persuasion.

Over the course of the next three chapters, we dig into each of the pieces of the GAP Method in much more detail and show you how to apply it to each of your communication opportunities.

Ms. Brenner's History Class

A few years ago, I went back to school—high school, in fact. My wife, Emily, has taught history and English at Choate, a Connecticut boarding school since 2001, with a few pauses along the way to focus on full-time parenthood. My schedule was open one afternoon, so I visited her U.S. History class. I snuck in early, sat in the back row, and tried in vain to blend in—the wedding band, the flecks of gray hair, and the fashion choices that haven't worked since the 1990s clearly gave me away.

I was there to hear and see my wife teach, not to think about my work with The Latimer Group. As I walked into her classroom, I was not totally cognizant of the similarities between her work and mine. My world is about teaching persuasive speech and effective communication to professional adults. Her world is about teaching history to teenagers.

But as I sat there that afternoon, something struck me. Emily began her class by discussing the AP history exam they would all be studying for the following spring. She was reviewing the skills they would need to succeed. "You will be graded on two things—your command of the material and your writing ability. If you can't communicate with the readers and make your point, you won't get a good grade, no matter how much

(continued)

41

history you know. The examiners care about what you say, but they also care about how you say it."

That was excellent advice.

As I left the classroom, still looking incredibly out of place, I realized that some of the most critical professional lessons are available to us even at an early age. We spend an inordinate amount of time, resources, and money relearning some of the basic skills that have been available to us and were taught to us at much younger ages. Emily's message was the perfect one for her students. And I suspect a few of her students' parents would also benefit.

Professional success can be reduced to a few key skills, one of them being the ability to articulate and deliver your message. This ability serves us well in every company and industry in the modern business environment. All of us are more likely to excel if we can communicate—even high school history students.

There certainly are differences between the classroom and the boardroom—no detention for one, and a more consistent dress code for another. But the basic requirements for success are remarkably similar. Emily's students may soon forget the five U.S. presidents who were never inaugurated, but let's hope they remember the importance of articulate expression.

3

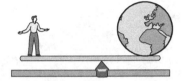

The GAP Method, Part I: Identify Your Goals

It usually takes more than three weeks to prepare a good impromptu speech.

—Mark Twain

The GAP Method begins, literally and figuratively, with a discussion of our goals. We live in a goal-oriented society, but time after time I work with organized, successful individuals who do not fully incorporate their goal-setting into their everyday work. To illustrate the point, here is an example of a real conversation I had with a client of The Latimer Group:

> *Mary:* I'm not getting the results I want. My sales production should be better.
>
> *Dean:* What do you think the problem is? Are you working hard?
>
> *Mary:* First one in the office, last one out, every day.
>
> *Dean:* Are you getting out of the office, meeting people and networking? Do you follow up with people?
>
> *Mary:* All the time.
>
> *Dean:* Have you set some goals for yourself?
>
> *Mary:* Definitely. I set monthly, quarterly, and yearly goals for production.
>
> *Dean:* Sounds like a good thing to do. Now, tell me about a typical sales call. How do they usually go?
>
> *Mary:* Fine. They always seem to go fine.
>
> *Dean:* Just fine? Not great? Let me guess—you don't make the sale often enough?
>
> *Mary:* No, I don't.

Dean: What's an example of a typical goal you have set for yourself before you give a presentation to a room full of prospects?

Mary: I'm not really sure.

I have had many similar conversations throughout my career as a communication coach. This may surprise you, but despite the fact that we live in a competitive, goal-oriented society, our goal-setting habits usually do not trickle down below the monthly, quarterly, or yearly evaluations. Many people are frustrated by their inability to persuade their audience to close the deal, make the sale, receive the grant, or win the case. Yet a shocking number of these same people admit to not having short-term or immediate goals for their persuasion opportunity. Often they lack a basic coherent answer after being asked, "When you walk out of the room or hang up the phone, what do you want your audience to think or do?" This is not a complicated question, yet most people don't take the time to answer it. But once you do, you will immediately recognize the outcome.

Persuading people to subscribe to your way of thinking or to buy what you are selling is difficult because convincing someone to think differently about a topic is no easy task. But persuasion becomes infinitely more difficult if we don't follow a defined method and prepare to succeed. The first step toward successful persuasion occurs before you get anywhere near your audience: you have to decide what outcome you want. Sometimes this first step occurs in your head or in a conversation with colleagues. Write the answers down or brainstorm them on a white board, but

Figure 3.1 What are you trying to do? What are you trying to achieve?

this first step has to occur—somewhere, someway. At some point, you must ask yourself, "What do I want to achieve in my meeting (or presentation, sales call, pitch, class, closing statement, or interview)?" (See Figure 3.1.)

Asking what outcome you want is incredibly simple, but how can we achieve a successful outcome without first defining for ourselves what we mean by success? While we are in the business of defining things, let's start by defining *success*. It means different things to different people, but in a professional context here's a good, basic definition: "An event that accomplishes its intended purpose."

Training for the Olympic Team

Defining success and goal-setting were important parts of my life when I was training for the 2000 U.S. Olympic

47

Sailing Team. My teammates and I spent six years training for the Olympic team, and the entire program was directed toward winning the Olympic Sailing Trials. In the United States, the only way to make an Olympic team is to win the trials in your sport. In other words, we spent six years training to win one regatta. While we were doing this, all three of us on the boat had other things in our lives such as careers and family. We trained hard and we trained frequently. In my case, I had a high-pressure career as a financial advisor at a major financial services firm, and at the same time spent significant time training on the water. In the early years, we spent approximately 75 days training, away from our careers. Toward the end, we spent close to 180 days on the water. For the final few months, we were on sabbatical from our jobs to focus on our training full-time.

Obviously, goal-setting was important to our success. Without an ability to manage our time effectively and analyze our progress, it would have been hard to successfully juggle the things in our lives and keep all the balls in the air.

The one lesson we learned over and over again was the importance of setting goals for even the smallest things we did. We had big-picture and long-term (macro) goals (i.e., win the trials and a gold medal), and we had more detailed and short-term (micro) goals as well (i.e., produce a better result at the next regatta next month). Eventually, we learned the importance of setting even more micro goals, and began setting them for every practice session, every day. Since time was in such short supply for us, we needed ways to gauge how well we were spending our time. For example, every time we practiced, we never said we would practice for "five hours." Instead, we would say that we would practice until we perfected a certain maneuver. If we perfected that maneuver in one hour, we were done. If it took us eight hours to perfect it, then we practiced for eight hours.

Big-picture goals are never enough, and setting both macro and micro goals is critical. We call this having multi-layered goals. Having multiple types of goals will facilitate long-term progress and success. Some people say, "Don't sweat the small stuff," and I agree that in some parts of our lives, letting the small stuff slide is important. But when it comes to goal-setting, the "small stuff," such as daily goals and communication goals for each sales call, is equally important as the "big stuff," like the quarterly or annual sales goals.

Lesson 1: Create Multilayered Goals

Creating multilayered goals is the first primary point of this chapter. To give yourself the greatest chance to persuade your audience, you must first be absolutely clear in your own mind how you define success, and what the goal for the communication opportunity is. Setting goals is required. We all know that. As a professional culture, we do a great job setting the big-picture goals—the monthly, quarterly, and yearly targets. But goal-setting should continue to trickle down into our daily lives as well and every persuasive opportunity should begin with a simple question: "What do I want my audience to think or do when I am finished speaking?"

49

Digging Deeper

The recognition that you have to set many layers of goals is important. But you also need to think about the goals themselves, and what makes a good, reasonable goal.

In my work with The Latimer Group, many of the people I come in contact with have goals of some kind. In almost all cases, the goals are related to the outcome. A sales goal, for example, is an outcome-oriented goal. If my goal is to double my production from last year, or to be the number one salesperson in the organization by the end of the year, then my goals are about the outcome. This is a problem, and not the best way to define your goals. Having goals is an important part of your professional success. You knew that before you picked up this book. I have also suggested to you that having long-term *and* short-term goals is an important aspect of goal-setting. But beyond those two requirements, we must also *create the correct types of goals.*

In almost all professional scenarios, as in life, there are some variables we can control, such as how we look, how prepared we are, how well we know our content, and if we are on time for our meeting. But there are many more variables that are largely beyond our control. We cannot control how well-prepared someone else is for our meeting. We cannot control the audience: Whether they pay attention, care about what we are saying, purchase our product, invest in our idea, adopt our strategy, or follow our lead.

While we cannot control outcomes such as these, we can directly influence them. We cannot force our audience to purchase our product, but we can influence the variables on which they will make their buying decision. We cannot force our audience to vote for our platform or candidate, but we can influence their decision by making a compelling argument. We cannot force our employees to believe in us as leaders, but we can demonstrate understanding for their situation, and communicate the direction of the company in such a way that the employees are more likely to get on board. There are many things we cannot control and determine, but we can always influence the outcome.

Setting goals based on variables we cannot control is a recipe for frustration and, potentially, for under performance.

Back to the Olympic Story

For six years, my team's goal was to win the Olympic Sailing Trials, qualify for the U.S. Olympic Sailing Team, and win an Olympic medal. But to win the trials, we needed to defeat other teams. There were many things in this equation that were within our control. We could control:

- How prepared we were
- How ready our equipment was
- If our accommodations were acceptable
- If we had enough rest
- If we were physically fit and had been eating well
- How much research we did about the likely weather conditions
- How well we functioned as a team
- Our communication skills as a group
- If we had the correct coach

But for every variable that was within our control, there were several variables that were beyond our control. Here are a few:

- How well prepared our opponents were
- If our opponents' equipment was sound, or if it would break down
- The weather—how hard or soft the wind would be
- The wind shifts during the race
- The decisions of the race umpires
- Outcomes

Sports—like music, dance, or any theatrical art—are performance based, which means the performance will always be a variable. If I am a singer, some days I will wake up and my voice will feel stronger than on other days. If I am a runner, some days my endurance level will be better than others. In our Olympic sailing campaign, there were many important variables that were well beyond our control. And we learned the hard way early on in our six-year training program that we needed to distinguish between the controllable and the uncontrollable when setting our goals. We made all the mistakes we could possibly make, and it was reflected in our early performance.

We had a good team, right from the beginning, with plenty of support, all the correct equipment, and strong talent. We felt we should have had good results right away. We practiced hard, but our results were pretty poor.

In an effort to identify the problem, we began working with a sports psychologist named Jerry, who helped us see an important distinction. Jerry began our first session by asking us about our goals. He asked us what we thought about when we trained and when we competed. None of us hesitated. We made it clear that we were very focused on winning an Olympic medal. We were goal oriented, ambitious, and proud of it.

Jerry listened to us and congratulated us on having goals. But he then told us that our intent focus on this type of goal was getting in the way of our performance. He made us realize that all of our goals were about "outcomes" and that many things helped determine an outcome that we cannot control. His point was that our goals were too closely connected to outcomes beyond our control and that we were setting ourselves up for under performance and dissatisfaction.

Lesson 2: Focus on the Task, Not the Outcome

Jerry's solution was simple: Focus on the tasks that lead to success, and let the success take care of itself. Set all of your goals for the things within your control, and ignore the things beyond your control. If you effectively prepare, you will increase your probability of success.

Our goals should never be driven by the elements we cannot control and rarely be focused solely on the *outcome*. Our goals should be centered on elements we can determine and on the tasks that will lead to success, rather than on success itself (see Figure 3.2).

Figure 3.2 Instead of thinking about the outcome, spend your time acquiring the tools and skills that will lead to the outcome.

Let's translate this into the world of professional communication. If you are in sales, you want to sell more of your product. But there are many aspects of the purchase that you do not control. If all your goals are about the outcome—"close the next deal," "double my production within 18 months," or "be the top salesperson in the firm by year-end"—you are creating goals that are dependent on some things that you cannot guarantee or control.

A salesperson taking Jerry's advice, therefore, might develop a list that would look something like this:

- Start each day by reading the newspaper and trade journal for news and ideas about my product or industry.
- Clearly articulate my value proposition within the industry—for me, my product, and my company.
- Generate five new sales leads per week.
- Send out five pieces of industry research to clients and contacts every week.

- Take a colleague or contact to lunch once a week to share ideas.
- Research each person I am scheduled to meet with ahead of time.
- In every sales call, make sure I have a clear idea of what I want the audience to think or do when I am done.
- Only ask for the order when the time is right—but always ask.
- Within 24 hours of a sales call, follow up with a note; within one week of a sales call, follow up with a phone call.

Each one of these goals is a task that a salesperson can control completely. If you look at this list of goals, they hit on all the key aspects of sales—know your product, service, and industry; be well-informed; communicate clearly; systematically generate leads; reach out regularly to clients and friends; and follow up.

This can easily be translated into other professions. None of these goals are focused on outcomes; instead, each of these goals is focused on tasks.

Back to the Olympic Story Again

Let's return one more time to our campaign for the 2000 Olympic Sailing Team. Prior to our work with Jerry, we had only outcome-oriented goals and under performed. After our work with Jerry, our goals were about tasks, rather than outcomes, and about what we could control, rather than what we could not control. Our goals rarely had anything to do with winning an event or achieving a certain world ranking. Our goals were all focused on the tasks of executing certain maneuvers more effectively or developing a specific, important skill set.

Our performance increased dramatically, and within one year, we were winning events and were ranked in the top 10 of the world. Jerry's input was probably not the only reason our performance improved. Perhaps we were just getting better, but our performance improved at a rapid rate. I am certain much of our improvement was generated by our different approach to goal-setting.

Persuasion is not telling people what to think, but shaping what people think about and influencing the variables on which people make decisions. In a persuasive situation, you cannot control what people think, how they act, or the other influences on their lives—what their boss said to them right before you walked into the room, or the budget restraints that were placed on them six months ago. You cannot control how they feel about your product or organization because of relationships with your predecessors, but you can influence what they think about you, the variables they consider when making their decisions, the report they bring back to their department or manager, and their perception of you. You cannot control your audience, but you can influence the way they think and immunize them against the flattery of the competition.

So as we leave our discussion of *goals*, remember these two points:

1. Long-term goals are not enough. You need short-term goals as well. You need goals for every communication opportunity you have.
2. Your goals should be about the things in your control and should be primarily about tasks rather than outcomes.

In the context of our Leverage Metaphor, think of your ultimate goal as the act of moving your audience. How high do you want to lift them? What tasks do you need to focus on to raise them to the desired level?

As Mark Twain suggested, seemingly impromptu speeches require a great deal of preparation. The GAP Method and our discussion of effective communication start with good goal-setting, but does not end there. It also involves Part II of the GAP Method—the importance of understanding our audience.

Mr. Torre and the Evil Empire

Like all good marriages, mine has balance. I am a Yankee fan and Emily cheers for the Red Sox.

The early years of our relationship coincided quite neatly with the resurgence of the Yankee-Red Sox rivalry, which dates back to the early twentieth century and has had several peaks and valleys over the past century. However, 2002 to 2005 was the apex of the sports rivalry. Both teams were good, and thanks to Major League Baseball's unbalanced schedule, they played each other 19 times per year and frequently squared off again in the playoffs. From 2002 through the end of the 2005 season, no two teams faced each other more, and they played to a near draw.

Beyond my obvious sports fanaticism, those Yankee teams provided a fascinating study in leadership contrasts. On one hand, the Yankees were owned by the late George Steinbrenner, one of the most egotistical, impulsive, and impatient owners in all of U.S. professional sports. He set the bar high for his team, demanding excellence and expecting a championship every year, but he also was known to create a tense and suffocating work environment for everyone in the Yankee organization.

On the other hand, the Yankees were then managed by Joe Torre, one of the few constants in the Yankee clubhouse in the late 1990s and early 2000s. From my spot in the cheap seats, Mr. Torre was one of the great leaders in professional sports at that time. He set the tone for his team, had certain basic rules for player conduct, and then stayed out of their way to let them win games, division titles, and championships. He understood that life in Yankee-land did not revolve around him.

Playing and working for the Yankees has always been the biggest double-edged sword in modern U.S. sports. If you wear Yankee pinstripes, you are guaranteed several things. You will: (1) have the best facilities, the most amenities, and the best trainers in your sport; (2) play in Yankee Stadium, which is filled with history, tradition, retired numbers, and championship banners; and (3) work with a team that will spare no expense to bring in any player who might help the Yankees win. (According to Red Sox CEO Larry Lucchino, the Yankees were at the time the "evil empire," evoking images of Darth Vader, the Soviet Union, and U.S. Steel.)

But Yankee players also dealt with Mr. Steinbrenner, who would criticize his own players in the media, openly court other players to fill a

(continued)

position on the team (even ones already filled by veterans and team leaders), and randomly choose the players he wanted to keep and discard.

One of the basic tenets of good leadership is about having a vision for your organization or your team, articulating it, and building goals and consensus around it. For the Yankees, Mr. Torre regularly demonstrated good leadership, using an uncanny ability to get a locker room full of star players to work together. Many players on the Yankees were baseball stars before they came to New York, but Mr. Torre built consensus, helping them all work together.

Mr. Torre also continually protected his players from distractions (allowing them to focus on winning games), the press in the world's media capital, and Mr. Steinbrenner's intrusions. He didn't criticize his own players in the media, unlike many other managers, and treated them like the professionals they were, giving them the credit when they won and never pointing fingers when they lost.

Those Yankees succeeded for many reasons, including nearly unlimited cash flow, but there are many teams with high payrolls that do not succeed every year. The Yankees have been one of the wealthiest franchises for many years, but they still failed to make the playoffs between 1981 and 1995. Money alone does not create success. There are many reasons the Yankees were successful during the Torre years, but one of the most important reasons was Joe Torre himself. His style of leadership and communication was rare, unselfish, and offers a great lesson for us all.

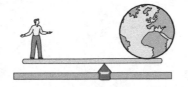

The GAP Method, Part II: Understand Your Audience

Talk to a man about himself and he will listen for hours.

—Benjamin Disraeli

You have set appropriate goals. You have decided what you want this audience to think and do after you are done speaking with them. You have a clear picture of what success looks like for you. You know where you want this interaction to go. Now the question becomes, "Where does this interaction start?"

Once we know our figurative destination, we must then think about our figurative starting point. If you are going to pick me up and drive me to work tomorrow morning at 7 A.M., there are two things you need to know—where to pick me up and drop me off. This is true in communication, too. If your job in our meeting next week is to persuade me of something, you need to know what I currently believe on the topic (i.e., where to pick me up) and what you want me to believe when we are done speaking (i.e., where to drop me off).

When we prepare to persuade an audience of something, the most often-overlooked aspect of the equation is our understanding of our audience. There is much we need to know, but when we know it, our goals become so much easier to achieve. Despite this, there is almost always much that we don't know, and often it is because we didn't even try. I am not suggesting that we need to think about our audience differently, but that, on an even more fundamental level, *we simply need to think about them*. Most of us don't take the time to think about our audience at all.

At the beginning of most new client engagements, I am often asked to help design a good speech or message.

My first few questions always revolve around who it is that we will be speaking with. More often than not this surprises the new client. Typically, I greet their surprise with the question: "How can we possibly know what to say unless we know what our audience cares about or what 'language' they speak?"

Steve, the New CEO

To understand the importance of understanding our audience better, it might be useful to consider my client "Steve" and his recent challenge. Steve called me because he had just been promoted to CEO. He was taking the place of a charismatic, beloved leader who had been with the company since its infancy. His predecessor had retired and the board of directors had decided that the company needed a different personality type to take it to the next level. Steve was a "numbers guy," very detail oriented and reserved. He was worried he would have a hard time meeting the expectations of the employees and matching his predecessor's sparkling personality. Steve was soon to be introduced to the employees, and he asked me to help him prepare for his first speech to the entire organization.

At the beginning of our first meeting, Steve began by outlining what he thought we needed to work on. Since Steve was highly organized, he had already prepared a draft of his speech. And since he was self-aware enough to know he was not very dynamic, he assumed we would spend our time working on his delivery and his style. But we did not begin there. I asked Steve for the speech draft. He sat there while I read it and took notes. His draft included the following pronoun frequency: 47 "I's," 22 "me's," 12 "you's," and *zero* "we's." The speech was written almost entirely in the first person, and entirely from his perspective. I cannot remember the title of his speech, but it might as well have been "My Goals, My Message, and My Vision." Steve's entire speech was about *his* situation and beliefs. There was little mention or acknowledgment of how the audience might be feeling, their perception of the transition to the new leadership, what they might be nervous about, what they might be excited about, or what their hopes and issues might be.

Meanwhile, Steve had a clear idea of his goals. He wanted to introduce himself to them, get off on the correct foot, and build a relationship with the employees. He knew where he wanted to "drop them off." But the concept of where to "pick them up" had never crossed his mind. His approach was egocentric, focusing solely on his desire to win approval, to express his hopes, and his desire to appear to have a vision.

Steve was at one end of the metaphorical lever that we introduced in Chapter 2; his audience was sitting out there at the other end. The fulcrum, the all-important point that balances the lever and determines how much power your words will have, was too close to Steve and too far away from his employees. He could jump up and down all day long on his figurative lever, but until he changed his approach, there was little chance he was going to be able to move his audience. He had no leverage. (see Figure 4.1).

Figure 4.1 You can try as hard as you want to... but if you do not understand your audience your fulcrum will work against you.

Looking into Hearts and Minds

Now is the time for you to look into your audience's hearts and minds and see exactly what it will take to move them from where they are currently to where you want them to be. As you prepare to communicate—create a speech, presentation, or sales call—understanding your audience will allow you to move the fulcrum as close to them as possible, giving you the leverage you need to be persuasive.

The good news is that looking into an audience's hearts and minds is not impossible. They are human beings just like you, so you already know plenty about them whether you realize it or not. If this basic knowledge about human beings is not enough (it usually isn't), your audience is often eager to help you learn more. All you need to do is ask.

If your audience is one or two people, you can get very specific about who they are and how they think. But as the size of your audience grows, you will need to make some informed generalizations.

As you attempt to persuade larger audiences, your understanding of each of them must be broader. It is not necessary, or even possible, to know each member of the audience as intimately as you would in a smaller environment. So the questions you ask, and the conclusions you draw, must be constructed from a representative sample. Sometimes, however, even in a large audience, there may be a few key decision-makers that must be persuaded if you are to be successful. So even though there may be 150 people in the room, your persuasive skills may have to be focused on one or two of them. Part of knowing your audience is to understand who the key decision makers are.

Move the World Audience Profile

Whether you are a high school student presenting a paper to your history classmates or a trial lawyer making your case, you need to build a profile to determine whether you will be able to successfully persuade the audience. Here is what you need to know:

- *Audience history:* If you are working with an organization that has experienced 10 consecutive years of strong growth and has recently gone public, you need to understand that history and why they have chosen to go public at that time. If you are working with a nonprofit that enjoys strong support from its community and is looking to grow beyond its area of name

69

recognition, you need to understand their historical strengths and reputation. If it's a company that has just gone through Chapter 13 bankruptcy or an individual who went through a tough divorce, it helps to know an organization's or a person's baggage.

- *Frames of reference:* There are many realities for an organization or a person, and many different frames of reference that influence what and how people think and respond. You'll need to select the ones most appropriate for your situation and your audience:

  - *Emotional:* How do you think the audience is feeling now and is likely to feel at the moment of your presentation?

  - *Financial:* If you are selling something, you need to know if and when they will have the money to buy it. What is their approach to debt? What have they spent money on previously?

  - *Ethical:* Are you trying to persuade scientists, students, churchgoers, or investors? You need to carefully figure out what your audience's world looks like and how they believe they fit into that world.

  - *Ideological:* What important beliefs does your audience hold, especially in relationship to what you are trying to persuade them to do?

  - *Competitive:* Whether you are trying to be persuasive in selling an idea or a product, you need to determine what competitive ideas your audience is holding or what their knowledge of the competition is. You also need to have some idea of the competition yourself.

- *Image of you:* What is your audience's sense of you? If they are going to be persuaded by you, they must first trust you. What is your current standing with them?

- *Perception of your ideas or products:* What is the audience's current knowledge and attitude toward what you are offering? Are they starting with a negative, positive, or neutral perception?

- *Point of agreement:* What common ground do you share with your audience? You don't need to agree with your audience about everything, but some common ground is extremely helpful.

- *Needs and desires:* Is there something that your audience wants that you can supply? What would your audience do to get it? How will they benefit once they have it?

- *Capacity to act:* If you are selling something, is your audience the decision-maker? If not, how many others are involved in the process?

- *Decision-making style:* Human beings make decisions based on fact or emotion. In any audience, some people will be more likely to be persuaded by facts, while others will want narrative stories and emotion. No one makes decisions based only on fact or emotion, so you will always need to have both ready to help you.

Truths You Can Bank On

There are a few fundamental truths about human nature that can help us better understand our audience.

People like to laugh. Laughter creates comfort, which usually leads to a level of trust. If you can make your audience laugh, you create a relationship with them and begin developing some credibility. But as we discuss later in this book, the use of humor only works if it is authentic. Don't force it.

People like stories because they provide a context that people can relate to, creating a sense of familiarity and comfort.

You know that people will make fast judgments about you and your integrity, whether they realize it or not. Your audience judges you constantly. From the moment they hear your name, or read your biography, or see you for the first time, your audience is judging you, deciding whether they ought to trust you, listen to you, or be open to what you have to say.

You know that if people do not trust you, you have little hope of persuading them of anything.

If they are members of a company, a school, an organization, or a community, they likely have some allegiance to the ideas, values, and cultures of those entities.

People believe that they are just and fair—and that their beliefs are true. If your goal is to change your audience's belief system or, at a minimum, have them consider the possibility that what you are saying might be true, then you need to first understand the enormity of your undertaking.

Most people resist change. Some are more resistant than others, but as a general rule, they need to be overwhelmingly convinced to think or believe anything new, especially if it is contrary to their current belief system.

Successful and busy professionals do not invest time and energy for small returns, so it is not worth your time and effort to attempt to persuade an audience of something small or marginal. If you do not attempt to move them off their current belief system in a significant way, you run the risk of a "so what?" response.

All of these things are true about every audience you speak to, whether there are two or two thousand people in the room. The net result of all these truths is that the stakes are high. Every time you stand up and speak, address a congregation, make a sales call, lead a meeting, or plead a case, the stakes are high. Your opportunity to capture the attention of your audience is fleeting at best.

The further you try to move an audience, the better you need to understand them. The greater the change you try to create, the closer your figurative fulcrum needs to be to your audience.

Your persuasion goals need not be (and better not be) a total recalibration of the audience's current belief system. This is one of the many ways all the pieces of the GAP Method depend on each other. If your goals are too ambitious, no level of understanding of your audience will make persuasion possible. For example, it would be difficult, if not fruitless, to try to persuade a Democrat to become a Republican, or vice versa, no matter how well you know them. It would be equally difficult (maybe more so) to convince a Red Sox fan to root for the Yankees.

Your audience will prefer to listen to, and are more likely to be persuaded by, people they like and respect. And they are making up their minds on whether they like and respect you from the first moment to the last.

Yes, the stakes are indeed high.

Try On the Audiences' Shoes

Taking the perspective of the audience is one of the most important ideas in this book. Most people, when attempting to be persuasive, make all kinds of assumptions about their audience (if they think about their audience at all) and just plunge right in. Imagine a child, "Jack," who wants a new skateboard—he will just go for it, not knowing or even caring if his parents have the money at the moment. Jack likely won't consider if his parents are worried about a broken wrist if they give him a new skateboard, or if his parents are focused on his recreational needs. The typical child will decide what he or she wants and will focus on that part of the equation.

But how much more likely to succeed would Jack be if he were able to find out first that his parents thought he ought to be helping out around the house more, especially mowing the lawn in the summer and shoveling snow in the winter? By discovering that, imagine how easily he could craft a winning proposal for that skateboard: "I've been thinking about ways I could help out more around here. Would you like me to start cutting the lawn every week? You don't need to change my allowance, but instead I'd like some help replacing my rickety old skateboard with a new Termite."

By simply taking the time to think about the perspective of the other people involved, you automatically give yourself the beginnings of a road map to persuasion and achieving your goals.

Very often, the power of persuasion starts with the power of asking questions and understanding your audience's perspective.

It's time to think about your specific audience. If you know the person or some of the people in your audience personally, you likely know much more about them and their beliefs. You may know some of their professional or personal backgrounds. You may know their investment history or sales tendencies. You may know the history and evolution of their company or organization. If you were introduced to or referred to your audience by someone who knows them well, you also have a direct pipeline to learn more.

What if you don't have a direct pipeline? How can you find out what you need to know about your audience? The answer is simple: ask.

Overcome the Fear of Asking Questions

Let's address the fears most of us have regarding asking questions of our audience before we even meet them:

Fear 1: We don't want to waste their time. Most of us hesitate to ask questions of a potential audience. Sometimes it is a concern about taking more of the prospect's time than necessary. But that concern is misguided. The surprising fact is that your audience, whether it's one person or a crowd of a thousand, wants the time spent with you to be valuable for them as well. No one wants time wasted, and if answering some questions will make the time more valuable for everyone, then all the better.

Fear 2: Our appointment will be cancelled. Many of us also hesitate to get back in touch with a prospect and ask questions because we fear that this additional contact may give the audience the opportunity to cancel, or because we might be seen as pushy. This is also misguided. If the prospect wants to cancel, he or she will cancel whether you contact him or her again or not. Don't let that deter you.

Fear 3: We may look like we don't know enough. But don't forget the converse of this fear. We also can look like we are diligent and conscientious about strong preparation.

Fear 4: We may be perceived as invasive. If we act invasive, we'll be seen as invasive. If we ask questions in a professional, respectful way, they will be taken as such.

Fear 5: We may compromise our improvisational communication skills. I have heard many people describe themselves as performing better in the moment, without significant preparation. But there is a big difference between being prepared and being scripted. I also prefer an improvisational approach and don't like being fully scripted. But improvisation is easier when you have reviewed your facts and can riff with the correct knowledge in your head. A fear of being overly scripted should never cause us to sacrifice our preparation.

Let's think about it this way. You have finally secured that important meeting with the prospect you have been pursuing for a long time. You want to make the most of the meeting that you worked so hard to get. So here is what you do. You call their office and say, "We are scheduled to meet next week, and I want to make sure that time is as valuable for you as possible. The more I understand about your needs and concerns, the more likely I will be able to explain how we can meet them. If I send over a few questions would you take a few minutes and answer them for me?"

You'll be shocked how often people will answer "yes." The questions cannot be too intrusive or take too much time to answer. And you need to make sure you are asking questions that will truly help you. You'll only get one shot at this, and if you waste your audience's time, they will never answer your questions again and they *are* likely to cancel the meeting.

Ask for the opportunity to e-mail a representative group—maybe six people who will be involved in the topic of your meeting or members of the organization who will be affected by the outcome of this meeting. Regardless, always position this request as a way to save time and make the meeting more valuable.

Once they have agreed to answer your questions, think hard about what you will ask. Insightful questions are the most powerful tools a speaker can have. There are consultants I know who make a successful living based on the use of a few precise questions. There are samples of these types of questions in this chapter and throughout the book. You will want to refine them and make them fit your needs. But once you get the questions correct for you and your goals, hold onto them and never let go.

Lessons from Steve

Remember Steve, the guy who was about to give his "hello" speech to his employees after the big promotion? When we last left Steve, he showed me a speech that was egocentric and ignored anything that his audience might have been concerned about. We then went through the steps of the GAP Method. Based on this new way of thinking, Steve came up with his own brilliant solution. He organized a small group of employees, and asked them some thoughtful questions. He spent time speaking with them in a relaxed environment, and soon he had a clear picture of what was on his new employees' minds. It turned out that, among other things, they had liked the previous leader, but the employees saw his departure as an opportunity for the company to focus on several often-delayed reorganizations that had been talked about for years, but never seriously attempted. The employees loved their old boss personally, but had become frustrated by his relaxed and seemingly disorganized approach to management. He told great stories, but the employees wanted more.

This shocked Steve, and he quickly realized that the organization was ready and waiting for the types of things he could bring to the position. They were enthusiastic about the same things he was. Steve took what he learned from this focus group and reworked his presentation. He spent less time worrying about the details of his delivery, stopped trying to be charismatic and a good storyteller like his predecessor, and focused on direction and substance and ideas for the future of the company. And he reorganized his message so that it was not full of "I's" and "me's." Since he now knew what his audience was thinking, he could speak in the first person plural—lots of "we's." He shared a vision that was aligned with their goals, and laid out an execution plan for the reorganization that the employees desperately wanted. Not surprisingly, his speech was well received, and it marked the launch of a strong partnership with his employees.

As we wrap up understanding your audience, here are some questions that were helpful for Steve. Perhaps you can adapt these to your own situation:

Audience History Questions

- How long has each person in your audience been at the company? Is this a relatively new workforce or an experienced and mature one?

- Do the employees enjoy working for this company? Is this a happy and motivated workforce or an unhappy and disillusioned one?

- What have they valued in past leaders? What have they wanted more of?

- What has previous leadership done to make employees' lives better? Worse?

Frames of Reference Questions

- How do employees feel about the current state of the company today and, in terms of the culture's productivity, the clarity of direction, the availability of tools and resources to get the job done, and the company's competitive status?

- What do the employees know about you, the speaker/leader?
- Does this audience need facts and figures to be convinced, or do they prefer stories that make things real?

The more questions we ask of our audience, and the more we attempt to learn about them, the more we slide our figurative fulcrum toward them, gaining leverage every step of the way. The more we move the figurative fulcrum away from ourselves, the more we adopt the mind-set of our audience and leave our own prejudices and opinions behind. We need to move closer to the thought process of others if we have any hope of persuading them to think differently. To gain leverage, we need to change our thinking and move our fulcrum. To gain leverage, we need to trade distance for power.

Knowing our goals tells us where we are going. Understanding our audience tells us where we are. Part III of the GAP Method—Create Your Plan for Persuasion—will help us connect these two points.

President Bush: Articulate Expression and the Perception of Intelligence

In politics, as in all professional endeavors, first impressions and perceptions are crucial for success. Regardless of how intelligent a person might (or might not) be, the way he or she speaks has a dramatic impression on the way he or she is initially perceived. When a person speaks well, people assume a certain level of intelligence. When a person falters verbally, people assume something else. Like it or not, people judge us initially based on how we speak and what we say.

The speaking skills of President George W. Bush have been debated and lampooned since the beginning of his presidency. I'm not interested in delving into the pros and cons of his presidency. Those topics are for other writers and forums. The intention here is not to denigrate the president, but rather to discuss the perception that his speaking skills create. There is no doubt that public speaking, especially when in an unscripted and uncontrolled environment, is not among his greatest strengths. The list of verbal missteps has provided more than a little bit of cannon fodder for the late-night television hosts. There have been a number of gems:

(continued)

- "The vast majority of our imports come from outside the country."
- "I am the decider..."
- "I will carry out this equivocal message to the world: markets must be open."
- "One year ago today, the time for excuse making has come to an end."
- "It's important for folks to understand that when there's more trade, there's more commerce."
- "There is an old saying that says fool me once, shame on...shame on you. Fool me...you can't get fooled again."

John Steinbeck once wrote that "we give the president more work than a man can do, more responsibility than a man should take, and more pressure than a man can bear." I would add to that list that we put our presidents in the spotlight more than any man should endure. As a result of 24-hour news, the modern U.S. president is in the public eye so often that it would be impossible for even the best public speaker to avoid making a few verbal fumbles. But the 43rd president's Greco-Roman wrestling matches with the English language take it to a whole new level.

I know many bright individuals who struggle to express themselves well, thus I do not believe that there is a direct correlation between articulate expression and intelligence. But there *is* a direct correlation with the public *perception* of intelligence and articulate expression. Our ability to succeed professionally is directly related to our ability to express ourselves articulately. We all want people to give us the benefit of the doubt. We all want to be thought of as intelligent, enhance our personal brand in the workplace, build credibility, and be taken seriously. One of the best ways to do all that is to express ourselves clearly.

Is President Bush intelligent? I have absolutely no idea. And the point is not to debate whether he is or is not. Until someone shows me an IQ test, I'll withhold my judgment. However, the perception of his intelligence is heavily influenced by the way he speaks. When he tells us that "we need an energy bill that encourages consumption," our eyebrows go up. When he tells us that "a tax cut is one of the anecdotes coming out of an economic illness," we wince. And when he says, "public speaking is very easy," we laugh—hard.

The lesson for professionals is that not everyone speaks brilliantly, but the ability to speak well is something we should all pursue and will benefit from. Eloquence and articulate expression

(continued)

remain powerful tools. These skills come natu-rally for some, and require hard work for others. Self-awareness is important when it comes to minimizing the impact of our weaknesses, but the importance of verbal expression, and the way it af-fects public perception, is crucial for success and has never been more important than it is today.

5

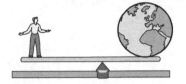

The GAP Method, Part III: Create Your Plan for Persuasion

A goal without a plan is just a wish.

—Antoine de Saint-Exupery

Many things contribute to professional success: hard work, creative thought, good timing, savvy analysis, and often a good amount of luck, to name a few. Most successful people admit that some degree of luck or being in the "right place at the right time" contributed to their good fortune. In my experience, however, nearly all successful people, organizations, product launches, and fundraising campaigns have a good plan, followed by good execution of that plan. At some point in the process, both planning and execution are required for a successful outcome. As the visionary baseball executive Branch Rickey once said, "Luck is the residue of design."

In the previous chapters, we have discussed the critical steps of identifying your *Goals* and understanding your *Audience*. We know the two points on our persuasive map: where to pick up our audience and where to drop them off. Now let's talk about our Plan: how we structure our message to connect those two dots and guide them from where their thinking is now to where we want their thinking to be when we are done. Our next step is planning and execution so that we can make our metaphorical lever as long and as strong as it can be.

The Building Blocks of Persuasion

The key to effective planning is to start with a high strategic level. It's about taking a bird's-eye perspective to see both the starting point together with your desired goal and each of the steps in between. From our perspective, there are five steps that we refer to as the Building Blocks of Persuasion. Every persuasive communication plan should contain aspects of each step. Collectively, these five steps will be used to construct your persuasive message:

1. *WHAT: Create a vision for your audience.* The vision you create may be lofty and strategic, articulating an entirely new direction for your organization, or it may be more immediate and tactical, mapping the tasks necessary to complete an already agreed-on project. But you must explain what the end goal looks like to your audience. Help them envision what life will look like if they follow your suggestion. Make it clear to your audience *what* you are recommending. Make it obvious *what* the topic or the vision is.

2. *WHY: Make the vision and the audience benefit real.* Once you have created this vision for your audience, you must demonstrate why and how they will benefit from what you are suggesting. People are, at least partially, selfish. We need to see how something will directly benefit us, our team, or our organization before we will agree to support the idea. Make it clear *why* the audience should follow your suggestion and *why* they should care about your topic.

3. *HOW: Provide the necessary details.* It is critical to demonstrate how your plan will work. If you are selling a product, explain the relevant features, costs, and/or the processes for closing the sale. If you are mapping out the completion of a project, explain

the details of the timeline, necessary steps, or likely issues that may arise. Answer *how* your suggested vision will affect the audience and *how* it will get accomplished.

4. *WHY NOT: Anticipate and resolve likely objections.* One of the biggest mistakes made during a persuasive situation is to ignore the obvious reasons why your audience may say "no thanks." When you can correctly identify the audience's potential roadblocks, the worst thing you can do is ignore them. If you can identify the resistance points, you should put them right on the table, address them, and work hard to shift the conversation to other variables or advantages. Here is a basic example: If you are not the low-cost provider in your industry, and you know that your prospect is price sensitive, the worst thing you can do is try to sell them without ever mentioning price. Your persuasive challenge is to cause them to make their decision on something other than price, like value. Don't ignore this crucial characteristic of the persuasive opportunity.

5. *WHAT NEXT: Map out the next steps and your call to action.* How many times have you walked out of a meeting without knowing what would come next—who was responsible for what, what the timeline would be, who would follow up, or when the next meeting was to be scheduled? Every persuasive message should include some detail about what will follow, including the steps you will take, what you want your audience to do, or the ideas you want them to think about.

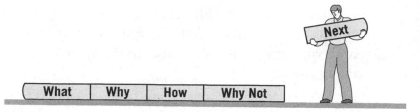

Figure 5.1 As you construct your message and build your Plan, the five Building Blocks are the critical pieces.

There are many ways we communicate in the professional world. We give formal speeches; make presentations with visual aids; make sales calls; participate in panels and town hall meetings; meet one on one, as teams, and in large groups; and communicate through the media. Regardless of the way in which we communicate with our audience, the previous five rules apply. They are the Building Blocks of our effective, persuasive communication plan.

Once we have sketched out these five Building Blocks to our message, we can begin to piece them together in a logical way. We can lay them out in a storyboard format, filling the necessary details for each of the five boxes (see Figure 5.1).

Important Aspects of Your Plan

Beyond the five Building Blocks, here are six other items you should think about as you plan your message to persuade your audience:

1. *Pick your 25 percent.* Whether your audience consists of 5 or 500 people, have you ever wondered how much of your message they actually retain? There are many studies that suggest that the human memory retains only a fraction of what it hears, even if the speaker does a great job communicating, and even if the audience is fully engaged. It is an often-quoted statistic that your audience will remember no more than 50 percent of what you say at the moment you are finished. And it is also commonly believed that twenty-four hours later, your audience will remember a maximum of half of that 50 percent. The point here is not to settle on the exact amount the audience will recall. The point here is to demonstrate that your audience won't remember everything, and twenty-four hours later they will remember a lot less. Regardless of the actual percentages, the reality is important for you to know.

   For the purposes of this discussion, let's assume that your audience will remember no more than 50 percent the moment you are finished, and no more than 25 percent the next day. Whenever I discuss this reality with clients, the initial reaction is disappointment and perhaps a little intimidation. But I like knowing about this reality because it forces us to be selective in our messaging, and it forces us to make choices about what is most important.

   So, if your audience is apt to remember no more than 25 percent of what you say, pick the parts that are most important and make sure they remember the things *you believe are the most important.* Highlight the

91

information you believe is critical to your success and make sure that information is prominent in your story. Make sure it is repeatable and memorable.

2. *Don't keep your audience in suspense.* Professional communication is not a movie. Movies may hint how the story ends, but their goal is to keep you in suspense until the end. This is what we expect and want in movies, but this is not what we expect and want from our professional communication. The vast majority of the presentations, speeches, and sales messages I hear do not highlight the main point early enough in the communication. Tell the audience the end point, and then backtrack and build a persuasive case to support your point. There is nothing more frustrating than sitting in a presentation for 15 or 30 minutes (or longer), with no idea where the speaker is taking the audience. Tell your audience where you are taking them.

3. *Can you clearly articulate your main point?* Let's say you are running a meeting tomorrow or giving a presentation next week. I see you in the elevator at the office and ask you what the meeting or the presentation is about. If you can't tell me the essence of the topic, it means you don't have your message tight enough. I am not, however, suggesting that every topic is simplistic enough to reduce down to one or two sentences. Most topics are more complicated than that. I *am* suggesting that if you cannot describe for me the essence of your main point or recommendation, or the essence of what you need from me, *then your message is not organized*

92

enough. If you cannot articulate the key points of your message in a couple of sentences then your presentation, speech, or meeting agenda is likely to ramble and stray. A tightly organized message still allows you to elaborate and build complexities, and it shows that your thoughts are fully organized and that the time will be valuable for all involved.

4. *Can you clearly articulate the supporting points?* When you have clear goals and main points, when you fully understand the issues and concerns of your audience, and when your plan is fully organized, you will be able to say: "In our meeting next week, I will recommend that we make the following choice, for the following three reasons—one..., two..., and three." Concisely stating the supporting points to your main discussion is clear, powerful, and persuasive.

5. *Design an opening that grabs attention.* We need to capture the attention of our audience right away, lest they become disinterested and begin thinking about something else. So what will grab their attention? That depends on the nature of your audience. But take your pick from a compelling statistic or fact, an engaging story, an appropriate quote, analogy, or metaphor. Make sure whatever you open with connects somehow with the main point of your message and does more than tell an unrelated joke, or share a story about the flat tire you got on your way to the meeting. Whatever you open with, make it matter, and make sure it connects to the message you are about to share.

6. *Design a close that is powerful.* This is directly related to picking your 25 percent. Because your audience is most likely to remember what you last told them, make sure you close with the most important aspect of your message. Returning to our Building Blocks of Persuasion, a good close repeats the WHAT (a clear statement of the main point, the key request or recommendation), the WHY (why the audience should care or why they benefit from what you are recommending), and the WHAT NEXT. A good, powerful close does not need to be long. It should be clear and brief, simply repeating the things you most want your audience to remember—WHAT, WHY, and WHAT NEXT.

Bringing It All Together

Now that you have the basic Building Blocks of your message—the WHAT, WHY, HOW, WHY NOT, and the WHAT NEXT—you have the necessary pieces to storyboard a powerful message. Once you have thought about the most important 25 percent, articulated your key point and primary points of support, and designed a powerful opening and close, you have everything you need to build a powerful, compelling message (see Figure 5.2).

Persuasion is not always easy. Convincing people to change their minds or behavior is hard. But if you take the time to think about the essence of the GAP Method—know your Goals, understand your Audience, and then create a Plan to change their thinking—you dramatically increase your chances for success. Guaranteeing success is a

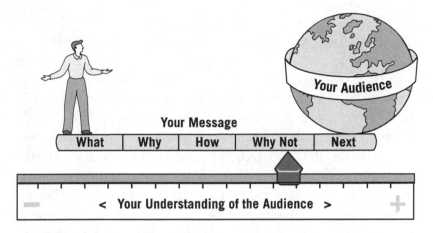

Figure 5.2 When you understand your audience and construct a good message, lifting up your audience becomes significantly easier.

loser's game in any industry. I don't guarantee perfection, but I do guarantee that the GAP Method will give you a great chance every time. I've seen it happen over and over again.

Jason, the Stockbroker

I recently worked with a young broker at a major financial services firm who we will call "Jason." He seemingly had all the skills you would want in a salesperson—personality, presence, a strong voice, confidence, and a good working knowledge of his industry and his products. Jason hired me to help him because he had been struggling to reach the next level of production at his firm. His career was stalled, and he wanted to achieve greater performance.

95

After spending some time together, it quickly became apparent that Jason's greatest skills were also his biggest liability. He had terrific "natural" sales skills. He had the aura, the look, and the confidence. People liked him. He was knowledgeable, a great conversationalist, and charismatic. But he tended to rely on these natural skills far too much. A brief conversation about Jason's past revealed that he had always been able to succeed based on his natural abilities without needing much preparation. Perhaps because of his strengths, Jason had never focused on creating a plan for success. In his current job, he had never even thought to create a plan to persuade his audience and sell his product.

His skills and natural abilities helped him graduate from an elite MBA program at a top university and to secure a position at a major financial services firm. His skills and natural abilities had taken him far. But he was now playing in the "big leagues," and Jason's natural skills were not enough to distinguish himself from the competition in his firm and at other firms. The stakes were higher and the competition was more intense. Jason was attempting to compete in the world of multimillion-dollar endowments, wealthy individuals, and sophisticated, successful people. Persuading an institution to let you manage their $250 million endowment is no easy task, and there are plenty of other eligible suitors available. Convincing a sophisticated couple to let you manage their family trust, their retirement fund, and the money they have saved for their child's college tuition is a tough sell. His natural skills, personality, and confidence might be enough to get him in the door to this world, just as those things had been enough to help him succeed in college and graduate school.

In the end, to move to the next level of production and earn the right to *stay* in this world, Jason had to be willing to create a strategy—a focused plan to get from Point A to Point B. He needed a plan for success.

We completely changed Jason's sales approach. We used the five Building Blocks of Persuasion to identify the most important 25 percent of his message and how to articulate it in a clear and compelling way. Instead of looking only at his delivery skills, we focused on his plan and strategy. We spent zero time on his delivery, speaking style, body language, or look. Instead, we pushed Jason to formalize his sales communication process. We worked with him on setting goals, and we opened his eyes to the critical information he needed to learn about his audience.

Lessons from Jason

Setting goals and learning about the audience were not foreign concepts to Jason. He had heard these sorts of things before, but he simply had set the wrong type of goals and asked the wrong questions about his audience. Instead, we worked with Jason to answer the important questions: Why had clients purchased his company's product in the past? For those who had not purchased, what were their roadblocks or objections? What was the market's perception of Jason's company and their product?

Once Jason was able to answer these questions, we could craft a communication plan that played to the strengths of his company and product and that directly addressed the objections of potential customers. Jason determined that his audience perceived the price to be too high for the product. Our plan centered on shifting the customer's focus from price to value. To force that shift toward value, the plan highlighted the benefits to the audience that competing products did not provide. As long as Jason allowed his audience to remain fixated strictly on price, then he would lose the majority of the business he competed for. Regardless of his natural sales skills (of which he had many), Jason was destined to under perform until he formalized his plan and his approach to selling.

Natural Skills versus Good Preparation

A good handshake, great conversation, and an outgoing personality are often the traits that cause us to tag someone as a "natural salesperson." But I find this misguided. Sales success is almost always dependent on the ability to persuade the audience to think a certain way. A successful salesperson is methodical in his or her approach and employs a plan for success. Many successful salespeople possess some of the traits that Jason exemplified, but that is only the beginning. Success requires much more than any natural skills that we may be blessed with.

As I have mentioned, I am a baseball fan, and here's a good analogy to illustrate my point. Every time a player moves up to a higher level of the game—little league to high school to college to the many levels of the minor leagues, and ultimately the majors—there is a greater contration of talent. At each new level, there are more good players competing for fewer spots, and hard work is required to a greater degree. At the major league level, everyone is a great baseball player. What distinguishes the great from the very good and the very good from the merely good is often work ethic and attention to detail. There are very few players who have long, successful careers in major league baseball on talent alone. Talent and natural ability can get you in the door, but to stay there, hard work and a plan for success are required.

You can find countless other analogies to illustrate the same point. Jason had the ability to move up several levels, but once he got to the major leagues—a good position at a high-end financial services firm competing for business from sophisticated clients—he needed a plan to stay there and thrive. The GAP Method provided him with exactly that.

Another way to think about Jason's mistakes is to think about the difference between strategy and tactics. Previously, Jason had focused on decisions in the moment (i.e., tactics) and rarely considered decisions ahead of time (i.e., strategy). He typically relied on his skills in the moment to lead him to success and rarely spent time planning ahead. As we see in the next section, individuals and organizations need a balance of strategy and tactics to reach the finish line ahead of the competition.

Balancing Strategy and Tactics

As you may have figured out by now, the sport of sailing is an important part of my life. I spent six years training for the 2000 Olympic Sailing Team and came close, but did not qualify. After that experience, I spent part of my time steering the U.S. Olympic Sailing Program as its chairman and team leader.

Olympic-level competition is incredibly high, in all sports. In my sailing experience, nearly every serious competitor is a world-class sailor, in excellent physical condition, and has spent countless hours perfecting technique, speed, and maneuvers. Because of the competitive nature of both Olympic-caliber sailing and professional industries, I often draw parallels between the two in my writing and client work. Both require certain intangibles: vision, determination, confidence, and patience. There are tangible requirements as well: mastery of skills, teamwork, effective marketing, financing, organization, first-rate communication, and sales skills.

But the one similarity between sailing and business I find most intriguing is the necessary balance between strategy and tactics. Olympic-caliber teams are masters of both, and they understand the nuances required to balance strategy and tactics.

Let's look at a dictionary definition of the terms:

> **Strategy:** the science of planning and directing operations, specifically of maneuvering into the most advantageous position prior to the actual engagement with the opposition.
>
> **Tactics:** the science and art of maneuvering resources in action or in response to the competition.

In a more practical sense, your strategy is your pregame plan to achieve your goal. Tactics are the decisions you make and how the strategy is altered in response to changing conditions during the game.

Prior to beginning a sailboat race, competitors determine their race strategy, which in its simplest form consists of a plan to cross the finish line first. Sailors look for the best wind and the most advantageous conditions. Businesses and companies do the exact same thing. Executives plot a communications plan, which generally consists of a brand strategy, product launch strategies, and business development strategies, all designed to gain an advantage over the competition.

On the race course, once the race begins, a natural shift from strategy to tactics occurs. Some teams will execute better than others, forcing competitors to adjust their plan. Perhaps the wind, water, and/or weather will change, making the chosen strategy less appropriate. Perhaps it will become apparent that the pregame strategy was flawed. Whatever the case, the best teams adapt their prerace strategy by making tactical decisions in changing environments to achieve their goal.

Good strategy and good tactics together are required for success—on the water, in the boardroom, on the shop floor, or in a sales meeting. Strategy without tactics leads to inflexibility. Tactics without strategy leads to disintegration. Metaphorically, strategy without tactics will cause you to keep racing north when your opponents all have identified a wind shift and are now sailing east. And tactics without strategy will cause you to change directions, repeatedly causing you to lose sight of the bigger picture.

I am taking you down a path of discussing strategy and tactics because strategic planning generally occurs in the senior levels of an organization, but tactical decisions are best made in a more responsive, agile way. Often, the market or the client asks questions or presents scenarios that require an immediate response, and there may not be time to defer the issue through the channels of the organization. The marketplace and the customer often require a rapid response. While the senior executives can and should play the role of strategist, the managers and sales teams often are the organizational tacticians. The sales teams and managers are at the front line with the customers, implementing the strategy day-to-day and giving it a face and a voice. They are the ones who need to react quickly to the customer's questions or comments.

In Jason's case, he needed a strategic plan and the ability and resources to respond, no matter what the situation, with tactics that make sense. But some of you reading this book are not on the front line with the customers. Some of you are managers and executives, more removed from the front line. Part of your plan must be to empower your people on the front lines, like Jason, and give them the tools and the authority to react tactically. You may set the organizational strategy, but Jason is your tactician. Many organizations spend generously on strategic planning and organizational branding. But often, the investment does not trickle far enough down into the organization. Although great investments are made on the strategic plan, comparatively little is invested to make sure your tacticians can capably articulate the persuasive message and branding that you have invested in so heavily.

How do you avoid making this mistake in your organization? How can you help Jason be the best tactician possible? Here are a few things to think about:

- Have you put in place the proper training to make sure all your people can articulate the company message in a consistent and compelling way?
- Are you confident that the people throughout the organization are capable of bringing your strategy and message to life with their words and their actions?

If your answers to either of these questions are at all unsure, there are three things you should consider:

1. Everyone should be educated on the strategic message so that they can understand and articulate it in a consistent way.
2. Your message should be layered so that there is substance, texture, and context to it. It is not enough to simply say "customers are our top priority." There needs to be sufficient layers so that the message can be brought to life by individuals throughout the organization.
3. Empower individuals throughout the organization with sales skills and tools to allow them to convey the organization brand—through their words and actions—in a way that is consistent and enhances the ability to achieve the strategic goals.

If you are leading an organization, your communication plan must include training and empowering your tacticians—

the Jason in your organization—so they can carry your message in the most powerful and persuasive way.

Motivating Your Audience to Act: Reason versus Emotion

Persuasion is not easy, as previously stated throughout this book. Each of us possesses our own beliefs, experiences, preferences, and prejudices. Convincing someone, through verbal communication, to adjust to your way of thinking can be daunting, and it is even more difficult to motivate a person to take the next step and *act*. If influencing thought is hard, persuading action is considerably harder.

But therein lies the real power of persuasion.

If I possess effective communication skills, I can be very successful in changing your thinking about my product. But unless I further motivate you to purchase my product, there is little measurable value in having changed your mind. Ultimately, my success depends on my ability not only to persuade you to think differently but also to motivate you to act on your new belief system.

Ultimately, the challenge is to leverage the power of persuasion to motivate our audiences to think *and* act differently.

In my role as chairman of the U.S. Olympic Sailing Program, I was ultimately responsible for leading a committee of 32 people that administered and supported more than 100 athletes who were preparing for the 2008 Olympic and Paralympic Games in Beijing, China. Our ultimate goal was simple: win as many medals as possible at the 2008 Games.

And the same was true after Beijing, when we repeated the effort for the 2012 Games in London.

Succeeding at the Olympic level of competition is difficult under any circumstances. However, that Olympic Sailing Committee inherited a program in a particularly tenuous position. Several competitor nations were outspending us by a significant ratio. Our athletes were competing essentially as amateurs in a quickly evolving professional world. Our medal count over the past three Olympic Games had started to dwindle, and fewer and fewer American sailors were choosing to put their lives on hold to train for future Olympic Games.

In the past, all of our athletes were responsible for raising the vast majority of the funds they needed in order to train. There simply wasn't any meaningful support provided by the Olympic Sailing Program. Therefore, the prospect of trying to raise hundreds of thousands of dollars from family and friends to be on equal financial footing with international competitors was intimidating to most American sailors considering a run at the Olympic Games. In other countries, the government often funds the Olympic Program. But this is not so in the United States. The athletes have to find ways to fund themselves, or their national governing bodies (like U.S. Sailing) have to find their own ways to support their athletes. Our athletes compete at a significant financial disadvantage in every Olympic sport. The prospect of competing against fully funded professionals was simply becoming too great of a financial and time burden for most U.S. sailors.

At the end of 2004, the U.S. Olympic Sailing Program had all the characteristics of a classic business challenge: declining output, shrinking revenue streams, intense international competition, and disgruntled employees. The program was in desperate need of some fresh thinking.

To reinvigorate the effort, the first order of business was to bolster our fund-raising program to supplement revenues. This would allow us to increase the number of athletes receiving critical support. Our committee did all the appropriate things called for by the GAP Method. We set several strategic goals and drafted a budget. We spent time talking to potential donors to find out how we could get them on board. Based on those conversations, we made our finances completely transparent and cleaned all the waste out of the program.

We began crafting a message that we felt would resonate with our audience. We identified the facts and figures and then produced a well-reasoned, logical, methodical argument for why the U.S. Olympic Sailing Program was a worthy investment and deserved donations and support. We had several experienced fund-raisers look at our story, and they found no obvious holes.

Charlie, the Fund-Raiser

Our fund-raising efforts got off to a good, but not great, start. We had some success, but not the success we were hoping for. Then I realized that I had been ignoring something so obvious that I literally laughed at myself for not seeing it sooner—I had missed the connection between emotion and donations.

The moment occurred after spending some time listening to one of the other fund-raisers on our committee, Charlie, speak to a group of potential donors. I was struck by how he was positioning our need. Charlie's case focused on the personalities of our athletes. He mentioned them by name, showed pictures of them, and described their experiences. Charlie showed video of them describing their Olympic dreams. He handed out quotes from them. And he even brought an Olympic hopeful to a meeting with a potential donor.

On the surface, Charlie's version of our story lacked what I perceived to be the essential facts and figures of the funds we needed. He made the discussion about Olympic sailing very personal: short on numbers and details but long on stories and anecdotes.

When our fund-raising team sat down to discuss our message and strategize, I brought up this notion of selling facts versus stories. Charlie discussed his tactics and his point was simple. The numbers and details are important, he told me, but people will be drawn in by the emotional connection to the cause of Olympic sailing. This discussion helped me relearn the importance of emotion in the persuasion equation.

We adopted this approach of connecting emotion and donations broadly. Our message became first about the athletes, their personal stories, interviews, photographs, and a touch of national pride. We added facts and figures to make the connection between our athletes and our goals, but we clearly led with the stories and only used data to back up the stories. We made our message consistent across the board: in our presentations, newsletters, and fund-raising letters. We detailed the accomplishments of individual athletes and then made the connection between a donated dollar and the effect it would have on the lives of these talented, young sailors. We have helped our donors and potential donors see the connection between their support and the likelihood of seeing the red, white, and blue up on the medal stand.

The results of connecting emotion with donations have been dramatic. In the years that followed, millions of dollars were raised and the program's budget increased dramatically. With a growing top line, we infused new energy into the U.S. Olympic Sailing Program, and created a whole new generation of talented sailors who committed to full-time training efforts. Our athletes produced a long list of impressive competitive results from 2005 to 2008, racing against the best in the world. And all of this culminated with a strong performance at the 2008 Games in China.

Lessons from Charlie

The lesson here is simple. If you want to lead your audience to think a certain way, use reason and logic. Reason and logic, facts and figures, are critical to the persuasion equation. But if you want to take the next step and motivate your audience to act, leverage emotion and a personal connection. Provide your audience with specific action steps to take and then explain how they will directly benefit from taking those action steps.

You need to demonstrate how your product, service, or organization will affect their life, how it will have a tangible impact on them, and how it will change their reality. You must make it real for the audience. This is at the heart of motivation.

Whether we are talking about fund-raising for Olympic athletes, motivating a workforce, making a sale, or persuading an investor, the equation remains the same. Persuade through reason. Motivate through emotion. In my opinion, those are two of the most important concepts in verbal communication.

Certain Outcomes

We live in a world overwhelmed by data and information. We are bombarded by information, 24 hours a day, seven days a week. The Internet, television, radio, and print news sources tell us everything we need to know, and much that we do not. We overwhelm each other with information as well. Thanks to e-mail, voice mail, mobile phones, and newsletters, we can reach each other and communicate more easily and more rapidly than at any other time in human history. This trend of easier, quicker access and more information will definitely escalate. Business, politics, culture, sports—you name it and we can hear about it anytime, any place, with lightning speed.

We are not only bombarded by information but also assaulted with opinions about what is happening in the world around us. We are attacked by those who want to interpret everything for us. We are spoken *at* all day, every day.

When someone speaks *at* me, I lose interest quickly. People like that are clearly most interested in their own words and opinions. But when someone speaks *with* me, I am interested. I am more likely to listen. If they show me the respect of seeking my opinion, I will show them the respect to seek theirs. Professional communication in our culture has moved too far in the wrong direction. Too many people, too many presentations, and too many sales messages are now designed to speak *at* the audience.

Given these realities, there are two primary and important outcomes from using the GAP Method:

1. *You and your message will be memorable.* How will you stand out amid the cacophony of news, information, opinion, and noise? Making yourself memorable is no easy task, but if you follow the GAP Method, you will achieve exactly that. Think about it this way: How many truly memorable communicators have you met in your lifetime? When we meet someone who speaks clearly, who has anticipated our issues, and who packages their message in an interesting and compelling way, we remember. We remember their names, the message, and the interaction. The GAP Method will make you memorable because your preparation will be obvious, and, perhaps most important, you will have clearly demonstrated to your audience that you have taken the time to understand them, that their opinion matters to you, and that you respect them. This will make you memorable.

2. *Your message will be digestible.* Delivering information in a way that people can absorb, digest, and act on has become a lost art. If you organize your ideas based on the five Building Blocks of Persuasion, and if you follow the GAP Method in your preparation, you are much more likely to have a message that is easy to follow,

understand, and act on. You will be clear, and your message will be compelling. If your audience can understand and digest what you say, they are much more likely to be able to act on it. Use the GAP Method and you'll find out that it is possible to move the world.

Be memorable and be digestible. These are two good outcomes. If you could exit every communication opportunity with the certainty that you and your message were memorable, and that your audience was able to digest your message, would you be pleased? Would you feel as though you accomplished your goals?

You will not be able to persuade everyone nor will everyone agree to purchase your product, follow your recommendation, invest in your idea, or donate to your organization. But by entering each communication opportunity with clear goals, a thorough understanding of your audience, and a thoughtful plan to persuade, you dramatically increase the chances for persuasive success. Your audience will recognize that you are prepared, that you know what you are talking about, and that you have thought about their issues. They will remember your name and your message, even if they are not persuaded by it. And if they like what they hear, they will be able to act on your message.

Until this point, this book has largely been about the creation of your message. We have examined your goals—how high you want to lift your audience. We have looked at the first two variables in your effort to gain leverage—the position of your fulcrum (your understanding of your audience) and the length of your lever (the strength of your message).

111

We have done so through an examination of the three aspects of the GAP Method.

In the next two chapters, we look at the third and final leverage variable, the weight or force you can apply at your end of the lever—in other words, how you deliver your message.

Warren Buffett: Fresh Air from Omaha, Nebraska

When I read something I think is well done, I keep it. I have files of newspaper articles, columns, and editorials, as well as piles of magazines and annual reports all over my office. Frequently, I will stick my hand in the pile, pull something out, and reread it. Recently, I pulled out a 2003 Annual Report from Berkshire Hathaway. In it I stumbled across Warren Buffett's "Letter to Shareholders" and was once again struck by the power of a strong message and how compelling effective communication can be.

Mr. Buffett's 2003 year-end missive is a case study in honest and clear professional communication. The writing is so good, I'll let Mr. Buffett speak for himself:

> And now it's confession time. I'm sure I could have saved you $100 million or so, pretax, if I had acted more promptly to shut down Gen Re Securities. [We] knew at the time of the merger that its derivatives business was unattractive....I, however, dithered. As a consequence, our shareholders are paying a far higher price than was necessary.

(continued)

113

What a breath of fresh air. No finger pointing for a mistake—other than at his own chest.

> In buying businesses, I have made some terrible
> mistakes, both of commission and omission. Over-
> all, however, our acquisitions have led to decent
> gains in per share earnings.

Mr. Buffett describes his success in an honest,
humble way. The "decent gains" he refers to are an
average annual increase of 22 percent in book value
from 1965 through 1993, as compared to 10.4 percent for the S&P 500. This is decent, indeed.

> Overall, we are certain Berkshire's performance in
> the future will fall far short of what it has been in
> the past. Nonetheless, [we] remain hopeful that we
> can deliver results that are modestly above average.
> That's what we're being paid for.

In a world where 30-something investment
managers pound their chests over last week's performance, this is refreshing. Even though some
of the youth and inexperience on Wall Street
has been weeded out in subsequent years, there
is still a disturbing amount of misleading advertising. Have you ever seen a commercial for a
mutual fund company that contained a message
like this?

> True independence—meaning the willingness to challenge a forceful CEO when something is wrong or foolish—is an enormously valuable trait in a director....All eleven directors purchased their holdings in the market, just as you did; we've never passed out options ...[we] believe in honest-to-God ownership. After all, who ever washes a rental car?

Here, Mr. Buffett hits a Wall Street hot button. Everyone running his company, Mr. and Ms. Investor, is in there with him, side-by-side, and they are all motivated by the same things he is. He also made it clear that the directors are empowered to challenge him if they disagree with certain decisions. I don't recall ever reading anything like this in an Enron annual report. (Remember them?)

I could go on. There are plenty of other examples of honest communication and message clarity in Mr. Buffett's Letter to Shareholders— far too many to list here. In a world dominated by spin and marketing, this is indeed a breath of fresh air. And it clearly demonstrates the power and importance of effective communication.

CHAPTER

6

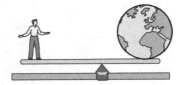

Gaining Weight, Part I: Build Essential Delivery Skills

If I were advising a candidate, I would say "Don't be so eager to be bright and quick and clever. Be you, try to be honest, speak with all the candor you can muster, and say it the way you'd say it to your family."

—Peggy Noonan

In my work with clients of The Latimer Group, I always try to understand the beliefs they hold about public speaking and effective delivery. I ask a lot of questions to understand my clients' (which is *my* audience) perceptions and beliefs. (I investigate Point A in order to take them to Point B.) The vast majority of the time, the discussion tends toward topics that I believe are not all that important.

Here is a typical exchange from my group coaching: "How many of you in the room today have ever had presentation or communication skills training before?" A few hands always go up. "And how many of you have ever read a book on public speaking, business presentations, or effective business communication?" More hands go up. "Quick. What is the first thing you remember from that class or that book?" The answers are always similar:

- Don't put your hands in your pocket.
- Use hand gestures.
- Don't move around too much.
- Make eye contact.
- Tell a joke.

Most people hold beliefs about effective communication that cause them to focus on the wrong things. It seems that at some point in time, someone, somewhere, decided there was an absolute correct way to speak in public, to be interviewed in the media, or to deliver a presentation. Because so many people believe there is one correct way to speak in public, there have been countless books written and classes taught giving us firm and unforgiving lists of delivery "dos" and "don'ts." Most of these beliefs are myths. Here are a few of the most commonly held myths about public speaking:

Myth 1: Be funny and always start off with a joke. If you've never told a joke in your life, please don't start now. You'll come across as unnatural. Be authentic to your personality, position, and message.

Myth 2: Strong gestures and body language add energy to your speech. This is not always the case. Strong body language can be very distracting. You should choose your hand movements carefully and only use them to punctuate key words in your presentation. Otherwise, you may distract your audience away from your message.

Myth 3: Never put your hands in your pockets. If you're going to jingle your change or keys in your pocket, true. But if it's not distracting to your audience, what's wrong with pockets? If you are more comfortable keeping one hand in your pocket, and the other one out, no problem. I do it all the time because it is natural for me.

Myth 4: Always use powerful eye contact. We definitely recommend *some* eye contact to engage your audience and assess their reactions, but there is no one correct amount needed. Eye contact is primarily about building a relationship with a person. You would not befriend someone who, when you were speaking with them, never looked you in the eye; alternatively, there is nothing more uncomfortable than forced, extended eye contact with one person at a time. Staring at one audience member will make them start to squirm, and that's not effective. You also would not befriend someone who never, ever took their eyes off you. That would be a little creepy.

In this chapter, I ask you to put aside everything you may have been taught about effective delivery skills. If you have memorized a list of firm things to do or to avoid, I ask you to ignore it for the time being.

Two Guidelines for Effective Delivery

Two important concepts in this book are that content matters and that delivery is a very personal thing. No two people speak exactly the same way, and the worst thing a coach can do is attempt to make everyone sound the same. I have seen people awkwardly using hand gestures and others awkwardly placing their hands in their pockets. I have heard people be effective with a booming, theatrical voice, and others be just as effective with a more soft-spoken, matter-of-fact voice.

There are two guidelines to keep in mind:

1. *Be authentic.* Delivery skills are the means, not the end. Think about fancy packaging for a product. You may be drawn in by the packaging, but ultimately the substance of the product will determine its success. Think

of your message as your product, and your delivery skills as the packaging. Nice packaging is important, but far less so than the product itself.

Each of us speaks differently and uses different mannerisms. Your delivery of your message needs to reflect your position and personality—and be authentically "you." We risk reducing our own credibility when we clearly adopt a different persona in front of an audience. How will they know what is real and what is not real?

2. *Do not distract.* A litmus test can be applied to evaluate effective delivery skills by asking: "Are you distracting your audience?" If the answer is "yes," then modify the distracting behavior. If the answer is "no," then you are already in the ballpark of being a strong and persuasive communicator. If you don't know whether you have distracting habits or not, ask a colleague for their honest opinion—and be ready to hear it. The bottom line is to do what comes naturally, as long as it's not distracting.

The delivery aspect of public speaking is a form of performance art. And like any other live art, your performance is variable. Some days you will feel better than others. Some days your voice will be strong, and you will be energized and look forward to your performance. Other days, you may be distracted, tired, or sick, and your performance will suffer.

Here's a good way to think of the performance challenge: While delivery is variable, your preparation of the message should be constant. You are always in control of setting your *Goals*, learning about your *Audience*, and mapping out a logical *Plan* to persuade. Therefore, like anything else that is performance oriented, if you control the constants and prepare as well as possible for the variables, more often than not, you'll be on the path toward success.

Speak in a Memorable and Digestible Way

I always encourage clients of The Latimer Group to strive for the following goals in the delivery of their message: Make your message memorable and digestible. Make it easy for people to remember what you say, and then make it easy for them to access what they remember about your message so that they can act on it.

Being memorable is a great goal. If you can make yourself stand out amid all the other information and noise, you have taken the first step toward successful persuasion.

Making your message digestible is equally important. If you can structure a message that your audience can remember, access from their memory later, and then act on, you have taken several more steps toward success.

So how do you make your message memorable and digestible? There are six things you'll want to keep in mind:

1. *Articulate your key point.* Can you clearly state the main point, recommendation, request, or finding? Can you simply and easily tell the audience what your message is about? If you cannot state the WHAT of your message prior to your meeting, presentation, speech, or

123

interview, it will likely not be clear to your audience. "Today we are here to discuss our team's recommendation that the company invest an additional $5 million in product development." If you cannot summarize your message that clearly, it is not yet clear enough. And, if it's not clear prior to your meeting or presentation, you have little chance of improving during the meeting because very few of us become *more* articulate and eloquent under pressure. Most of us stumble a little bit more when in the spotlight. So if you are not articulate or eloquent ahead of time, you may be in trouble.

2. *Articulate the primary supporting points.* Although you must articulate your main point, it is just as critical that the primary supporting reasons (i.e., WHY you are saying what you are saying, and WHY the audience should care) be clear also: "We are recommending this additional investment in product development for the following two reasons: First, we have a significant opportunity to outmaneuver our primary competition. And second, we believe the payoff from the investment will be at least five-fold." I am not advocating sound-bite communication. Most issues are too complex to be reduced down to a sentence or two, but it is critical that you be able to summarize the supporting points of your message in a clear and memorable way. Your audience will have this clear summary in mind as you guide them through the pertinent details they need to hear.

3. *Speak in bullet points.* Have you ever noticed the effect of seeing the main points of a letter or a paragraph

written in bulleted form rather than in longer, more prosaic paragraphs? Look at the layout of this chapter and other chapters in this book. What effect does listing the main points in bulleted form have? This way of writing ensures the likelihood that the reader will remember the key points. We write this way all the time, and we can speak this way as well.

Read the following two paragraphs out loud to yourself and ask yourself which speech someone listening to you is likely to remember more clearly:

- *Today we will discuss the GAP Method, which is a tool to help you persuade an audience. The GAP Method has three components: Goals are an important part of this method because you need to have goals to make progress. You also need to think about your audience and what they care about. And, finally, you need to think about what plan you are going to put in place to persuade the audience.*

Now read this out loud:

- *Today we will discuss the GAP Method, a powerful tool that will give you your greatest chance to persuade an audience. The GAP Method has three components:*

  One, identify your goals.

  Two, understand your audience.

  And three, map your plan.

Now let's discuss each of the elements of the GAP Method in more detail. First let's talk about identifying and setting goals... .

Do you hear the difference? When you speak in bullet points, you make it easier for your audience to focus on the important elements of your message, which then becomes easier to follow and understand. Your message becomes easier to digest, and you become more memorable.

4. *Speak in sentences with simple noun-verb construction, using strong active-voice verbs.* If you want to be memorable, work on shortening the length of your sentence structure. Many of us speak in long, drawn-out sentences with many subordinate clauses and lots of commas and punctuation. We make it hard for our audience to follow what we are saying. Instead, I recommend speaking in short sentences. Use powerful active-voice verbs and simple noun-verb construction. Here are a few examples:

- "We recommend investing..."
- "I believe..."
- "Our organization requires..."
- "Our goal is ..."

When you shorten your sentence structure and speak with simple construction, you make it easier to follow what you say, thus making your message more digestible.

5. *Provide internal summaries of your message and be your own narrator.* Think of yourself as the conductor on a train who reminds the passengers where they are on the journey—where they have been and what stops are coming next. You're a guide to your audience, leading them along the path of your story. Every once in a

while, remind them where you have taken them and let them know what is next.

6. *Don't forget the "what's in it for you," or WIIFY.* You should sprinkle WIIFY statements throughout your message. These are reminders or triggers for your audience to pay attention to what you are saying. Here are a few examples:

- "This is important to you because..."
- "This benefits you in the following ways..."
- "If you remember nothing else, remember this..."
- "Write this down, it's important..."

As a result, your message will be more memorable, and your audience will be able to digest and later act on your message. If your audience remembers your message, you stand a greater chance of getting what you want.

And if you do these things well, there is no such thing as "too short." No one has ever uttered the following phrase: "You know, Dean made some great points in his speech; I just wish it had been a lot longer." You will get to the point quicker, which will: (1) make you more effective and economic with your words, (2) make you more memorable, and (3) make the message more digestible. If you want to make a positive impact on your audience, take up less of their time and be more efficient with your words.

These are two goals you should remember every time you lead a meeting, give a presentation, or sit in an office on a sales call: Make your message memorable. Make your message digestible.

Create a Strong Presence

New clients often ask me to help them work on their presence in the room with clients or colleagues. They want to command greater attention and have more of the intangibles that are so obvious when we see them, yet are so hard to quantify. But just what do we mean by the term *presence?* It often begins with an obvious air of confidence—not arrogance. What does confidence look and sound like? Our professional culture often associates confidence with volume, physicality, and a crisply pressed suit.

Creating a strong presence is not always easy. There are certain things that cannot be added or subtracted from a person's being and presence. There are certain things that we are born with and therefore cannot be adjusted. We cannot change our height. A large physical presence can be a positive if used correctly. We cannot completely change our voice. While we can make improvements to our voice, it's hard to turn a mild, soft-spoken person into James Earl Jones. There are certain realities we have to live with.

But there are some things that can be done to increase our command of the room and provide us with more of that intangible we call presence, including:

- *Wait for attention before you begin speaking.* Have you ever attended a presentation or a meeting where the speaker or leader began speaking before their audience began listening? I have seen speakers be 60 seconds into their talk before the audience settles down. By then, the audience has missed critical information.

If you want to create a strong presence, you must believe that your message is crucial to your audience—and let your audience know it. If you don't believe your message is important, then why should anyone else? Show the confidence to wait until others are actually listening to you before you begin speaking.

One important warning—your words better be worth listening to.

- *Lead with an attention-grabber.* To persuade your audience, what you ask your audience to do or think must be valuable to them. Therefore, you need to begin making the request or the recommendation real to the audience as soon as possible. You need to find a story, anecdote, statistic, or quote that resonates with the audience, demonstrates what you are talking about, and relates to why the audience should care.

  If you are recommending a process change in your organization that will save money, try to find a statistic that quantifies how much money was wasted the previous quarter or year.

  If you are asking for investment dollars, try to capture the size of the market, the opportunity, and the potential return on investment.

  If you are asking for a behavior change, think about a story that demonstrates the impact the change can have.

- *Polish your opening to perfection.* Unless you are giving a formal speech behind a podium with scripted notes or text, you will most likely conduct most of your persuasive opportunities unscripted. Presentations, sales meetings, team meetings, road show events, and almost every other type of professional communication will not allow you to work off a word-for-word scripted text—but unscripted doesn't have to mean unprepared.

After you have waited for attention before speaking and chosen a powerful opening, you must have a lead-in that has been polished to perfection. Referring to the Building Blocks of Persuasion from Chapter 5, the WHAT and WHY of your presentation should be part of this polished opening. You should be able to tell your audience immediately what you are talking about and why it should be important to them. When this is polished, you immediately show your audience that you are prepared and should be taken seriously. A polished opening also will help you get beyond the inevitable nerves in the first moments of your presentation. It's not possible, or advisable, to memorize the entire presentation. And once you get going and warm up, you'll be more confident. By polishing your opening you protect yourself against an early stumble due to nerves.

You must walk into the room and immediately and clearly articulate the important aspects of your message.

- *Use appropriate eye contact.* Eye contact suggests confidence, whether you are speaking to one person in the hallway or 25 people in a conference room, and that you believe in what you are saying, giving you credibility. Eye contact allows you to build a relationship and helps people to listen to you more intently.

   As I shared earlier, there is no one right amount of eye contact. Guideline 1 says that you should do what is natural and comfortable for you, but if you are more comfortable with *zero* eye contact, then you are in trouble. Guideline 2 says that you should not distract your audience—and zero eye contact is very distracting—so some eye contact is required. Don't distract your audience with too much or too little.

Look people in the eye when you speak to them, and they will be much more likely to believe in you and your message.

- *Directly address members of your audience.* My definition of intangible *presence* is directly related to confidence. Confident people are much more likely to have a strong presence. Like anything else, too much of anything is a bad thing, so be aware that overly confident people can create a feeling of arrogance.

  Having *presence* means showing confidence. And one of the best ways to show you are confident in your speaking role is to engage the individual members of the audience and refer to them by name when you speak. If you know your audience well, and you know there is some aspect of your story or message that will resonate with an individual in the audience, then refer to them by name: "This new process will reduce the amount of time your shop floor manager will need to spend each week on managing his team, and I know this will resonate with you, Tom, because you've been talking for months about becoming more efficient on the floor."

  When you address members of the audience directly, they will be more engaged and listen more intently. And when you can engage them in a way that also reminds them of the benefits to them, you will enjoy an extra layer of benefit for yourself.

131

If you know your audience well enough, you can refer to them by name and engage them in the conversation.

- *Pause and repeat for emphasis.* One of my favorite verbal devices involves the use of silence. When you are guiding your audience through your message, make some choices about the most important aspects of your message, and look for some key moments to use a strong verbal device for emphasis. The "pause and repeat" is one of the best, and it also is a great WIIFY device. Here's an example:

  > *Our product will reduce waste by 15 percent annually, which translates into a reduction in costs of $1.5 million over the next two years.*
  >
  > *LONG PAUSE*
  >
  > *This is important, so let me say that again. If you use our product, waste will be reduced by 15 percent, which will translate into an extra $1.5 million back to your bottom line.*

  Use a correctly timed pause to your advantage, and say the important statement twice.

- *Display strong and confident body language.* Body language is one of those things that I believe is variable and needs to be authentic to you. Some people move around a lot when they speak. Some prefer to be more stationary. Either can be effective.

  It is important to convey your confidence as a speaker with your body language by standing up straight, with your shoulders square to the audience. If you are running a meeting sitting down, don't speak slumped back in your chair. Lean forward so you convey the appropriate sense of urgency and so that you can see everyone around the table.

Do what is natural for you, but keep in mind that body language is also a form of communication. Make sure you think about that and that you are communicating in a way that is consistent with your overall message.

- *Speak with appropriate volume.* This is a simple one. Make sure people can hear you.

Presence is an intangible variable, but we know it when we see it and hear it. Some of our characteristics or realities are not easily changed, but the previous list will give you more of that elusive but valuable currency known as presence.

Keeping Visuals in Perspective

The role of visuals and slides in a business presentation has become one of the most abused and misused methods of communication. When it is done well, it is a powerful way to enhance communication. But I daresay that it is rarely done well, and is most often done quite poorly.

Nevertheless, the use of visual slides is here to stay, so it is certainly a skill most of us need to have in our bag of tricks to succeed professionally. Here are a few important reminders for presenting with visuals in a more effective and powerful way:

- *Design the message first and the slides last.* All too often, people prepare for meetings or presentations by spending the majority of their time working on their visuals. Often, when clients of The Latimer Group need help preparing for a major presentation, they begin by handing me a slide deck, as if preparing the slides is the most important thing we need to do. How do I respond? I put the slides aside and start asking about the message and the story they want to tell.

The slides are merely a visual representation of the high points of the story you want to share with your audience. So, design the story first, and *then* develop slides that will help you tell that story.

- *You are the focus, not the slides.* This is an important mind-set for you when you are preparing your visuals, practicing your presentation, and performing. Always remember that your audience is there to hear you speak. They are not there to read your slides. So what are the implications of this suggested focus?

  - First, spend the majority of your time preparing what you want to say and what your audience will *hear*, rather than what they will *read*.

  - Second, during your performance, remember to keep your focus where it should be—on your audience. Their focus should be on you, and your focus should be on them. Too many nervous speakers turn their bodies toward their slides and speak to them, rather than to the audience. This is a big mistake. The best way to build a relationship with your audience is to face them and focus on them, thereby giving them a reason to focus on and listen to you.

- *Use clear and consistent slide headers.* Make sure your slides make sense. The longer your presentation or meeting, the more important it is that you divide your talk into chapters. Your slides should clearly match the chapters. For example, if you examined three possible solutions to the company's production problems, don't hesitate to use headers like "Solution 1," "Solution 2," and so on. Make it easy to follow your story, and easy for the audience to know where you are in the presentation.

  Clear slide headers will make your presentation tighter, more consistent, and look more professional. In addition there is also the practical reality that your audience of busy and distracted people may not (despite your best efforts) give you their undivided attention for the entire presentation. In this case, clear slide headers make it easier for them to reengage with you and the presentation when they check back in.

- *What story does each slide tell?* Explain what the slides *mean*, not what they say. All too often, nervous presenters will simply stand there and read the slides to the audience. If you stand up in front of the room and simply read the slides to the audience, take a guess how much value you, as the speaker, add to the presentation. You guessed it: not much. Use your slides as cues to tell a greater story. Use the words on the slides to launch into interesting and deeper information. The

135

slides should *not* include every single piece of information you want to convey.

- *Numbers do* not *speak for themselves.* This is similar to the previous point. Tell me what the numbers mean. What are the implications of the spreadsheet you are showing me? If you show me a rise in revenue, tell me why we have a rise in revenue so we can repeat it. Tell me if the rise is a permanent rise or a temporary one. If we show a rise in production costs, tell me what caused it. If you show me a need for more resources to finish the project, tell me why. Numbers are not self-explanatory.

  When you interpret the data or the numbers, there also is a practical benefit to you. You build your own brand as someone who adds value. If you simply stand in front of the room or sit at the conference room table and recite information, you add no additional value. Anyone can convey previously prepared information. But when you interpret the information, draw conclusions or themes, and share your thoughts, you add value that only you can.

  Build your own brand. Add value. Interpret the information.

- *Pictures are better than words.* If you can demonstrate a point with a picture rather than with too many words of text crammed onto a slide, your presentation will be more visually appealing and your story will be easier to tell.

- *Use consistent fonts, color schemes, font sizes—with a minimum font size of 28.* Another simple point. Make your slides look the same, with the same size headlines, subheads, and so on. If you can keep each bullet point to one line of text, it will force you to be economical with your words and keep your slides simpler. Your audience will read less and listen more. Ninety percent of the slides I see for the first time have about 50 percent too much text.

If you have a choice, also try to default toward simple fonts like Helvetica, Times, Times New Roman, or Arial. These are easier to read, more standard, and look more professional.

- *Use dynamic animation to introduce each bullet point individually.* You know what happens when you put up a slide with all the bullet points already on the screen? That's right. The audience reads all the bullet points before they begin listening to you. This means they start listening right about when you finish talking about Point 1. So, if you animate your slides, you will control what they read and your audience will listen to you the entire time. The goal is to be memorable, so make it more likely that your audience will continue to focus on your words, thereby making it more likely they will remember what you say.

- *Consider creating two slide decks—one to view and one to hand out after the presentation.* If you really have a significant amount of content that you need to pass along, here is a great solution to annoyingly busy slides. Remember, slides are meant to be viewed while your audience listens to you. They are not meant to be read. This is a subtle but important distinction. Yes, the audience reads the words on the slides. But you want them to view the slide quickly and then return to listening to you. So consider creating a much more

137

complete slide deck that you hand out after the presentation, for the audience to take home. During the presentation, you show them an executive summary slide deck with fewer slides and less content on each slide. Show them what they need to know in the presentation, and send them home with everything else. This is very effective.

These ideas are meant to do two things: First, they are intended to help you create better slides and approach your presentations with better skills. Second, and more important, these ideas are intended to help you keep this method of communication in perspective. Slides are an overused and misused method of communication, but we need to be able to communicate with visuals in a professional, effective manner.

Manage Stage Fright

Nerves and stage fright happen to all of us. I speak publicly and coach people on their skills for a living. I think about effective professional communication all day, every day, but I still get nervous before I speak. I am putting myself on display and there are risks when you are in the spotlight. There are professional implications, both positive and negative, for us when we stand up and speak. When we do it well, we are noticed, rewarded, and promoted. We are in demand. When we do it poorly, we also are noticed—for the wrong reasons.

Unfortunately, nerves are natural and they may never disappear for you. With that in mind, here are a few other thoughts that may help you increase your confidence and reduce your nerves when you speak:

- *Focus on the preparation, not the outcome.* This is an idea that comes directly out of my life as an Olympic-caliber sailor. When my teammates and I were training for the 2000 U.S. Olympic Sailing Team, we learned the value of putting all our focus and energy into improvement. We never worried about winning the event we were sailing in. We focused all our energy on preparing the best we could.

  Think about it this way. Success in your presentation is dependent on many things—some of which are within your control, while others are beyond your control. Focus all your energy on the things you can control, and over time you will condition yourself to think less about success and outcome. Use your energy to prepare your message, set good goals, learn about your audience, storyboard the message, create good visuals, and practice as much as possible. These are the things you can control. Spend less time on the things beyond your control.

- *Focus on the performance, not the outcome.* This follows closely from the previous point. Once your preparation is complete, don't go into your presentation thinking about a successful outcome. Think about the tasks required for a good performance and let the outcome take care of itself: arrive on time, make sure your handouts are ready to go, have your primary talking points clear in your mind, have a polished opening, be well rested, warm up your vocal chords, and so on. More often than not, success follows directly from good preparation.

139

- *Get into the space ahead of time.* This is a simple, but important point. Try to visit the presentation space ahead of the meeting. Make sure it is not too hot or cold, the technology works, and so on. There is nothing more stressful to a speaker who arrives in the room teetering on the brink of nervousness, only to find out that their laptop does not work with the projector that has been provided. Check that you have spare bulbs, extension cords, and so on. Leave nothing to chance.

- *Try to get to know the audience and speak with them ahead of time.* If appropriate, try to spend some time chatting with the audience ahead of time. It will calm you down, and you will get to know some names and faces—which should help you feel more comfortable in the presentation.

- *Take long, deep breaths to drop your heart rate.* Just before you go on, find an empty room or go to the bathroom and take several long, slow, deep breaths. Fill your lungs with air, hold it for a few seconds, and then exhale slowly. Do this several times to drop your heart rate.

- *Confidence comes from preparation.* Nothing will increase your confidence more than ample preparation of your message and practice. Make it a point to be well-prepared every time you speak. I get the most nervous when I am the least prepared. It is a pretty simple inverse relationship.

- *Confidence comes from proper focus.* If all else fails and I am still feeling some nerves, I remind myself that what I am about to share with the audience will be helpful to them. As a communication coach, I am often asked to speak at organizational conferences, sales meetings, and company events. Every time I am about to go on and I feel nervous, I remind myself that improved communication skills will help everyone in the audience and that if my audience absorbs my information, they will improve their communication. The net result of this mind-set is that I am focused on helping my audience, and not on myself. This always helps me relax.

We have spent the majority of our time in this book focused on how to create the most powerful message and how to prepare to persuade. But delivery of the message is also important. And while I do not espouse rigid lists of things you should or should not do, I do provide lists of reminders, suggestions, and guidelines throughout this book. Themes and reminders correctly applied will help make you a stronger speaker, a better presenter, and a more persuasive communicator.

The most important point to remember from this chapter is that you must be authentic in your delivery. Be yourself. Speak in your voice, with your own style, and you will succeed.

If you practice everything covered in this chapter, you will communicate more memorably, efficiently, clearly, and authentically. All of these things add up to an increased ability to apply greater force to your end of the metaphorical lever. You will create more leverage and credibility, the topic of our next chapter.

Politics in the Rear-View Mirror:
Candidates Gore, Dean, and Kerry

Election to the White House is dependent on many things, but chief among them is the ability to communicate clearly with your audience and the entire country. Politics aside, the 2000 and 2004 presidential elections gave us several examples of how inauthentic delivery or a poor and indecipherable message can limit success.

In the 2000 general election, our country was in the midst of a peace-time economic boom. To supporters of candidate Al Gore, this seemed to be his election to lose. Leaving disputes over vote counts, hanging chads, and legal appeals aside, the 2000 election should never have even been close. Mr. Gore lost that election for one primary reason—he failed to establish his own consistent and authentic voice. His audience could not identify who he was or what he stood for, and it cost him dearly. Though his message may have been a good one, his over reliance on public opinion caused him to alter continually his demeanor and delivery style throughout the campaign (and especially in those all-important debates). He never established a clear voice, an early wide margin shrank, and the rest is history.

In the 2004 Democratic primaries, Howard Dean gave us some fantastic examples of how *not* to craft a message. Here is the advice he desperately needed to hear:

- *Clarify what you stand for.* Most of what we knew about Mr. Dean and his message concerned what he was *against*—the war in Iraq, Washington insiders, tax cuts, George Bush. We rarely heard him discuss what he was *for*. His message was reactionary, with few clear policy proposals.

- *Make your message consistent.* It was ironic that he billed himself as an outsider candidate, yet he kept lining up yesterday's Democrats and Washington insiders such as Bill Bradley, Al Gore, Tom Harkin, and Jimmy Carter to endorse him. These endorsements clashed with his entire message.

- *Calm down.* His campaign events were often described as pseudo-revival meetings, long on excitement and emotion. In retrospect, they were short on detail and substance. We like our leaders to show they are human, but Mr. Dean seemed too emotional, too angry, and not balanced enough to lead us in a challenging world.

- *Lighten up.* In the 1984 presidential election, Ronald Reagan battled suggestions that his age

(continued)

143

was an issue. He effectively took that issue off the table in a debate with Walter Mondale by saying: "I refuse to make age an issue in this campaign, and will not exploit the youth and inexperience of my opponent." Everyone laughed, including Mr. Mondale, and the issue rarely came up again. Mr. Dean failed to demonstrate such humor and self-deprecation. He made some attempts late in his campaign, but it was too little, too late.

Finally, in the 2004 general election, John Kerry gave us other communication mistakes to dissect and discuss. There are a few things that are clear to me when I think about this election:

- *Electorates are like financial markets—they hate uncertainty.* At the time, my characterization of President Bush would have been simple. If he does anything well, he simplifies his message, making it crystal clear, certain, and memorable. You may not agree with his message—and many don't—but if you hear him speak, you understand and remember his message. Mr. Kerry continually failed to establish what he stood for—too many seeming position shifts. The message needed to be more clear, simple, and easy to understand. I watched his acceptance speech from the 2004 Democratic Convention *three times*, and I still had no idea what he was really saying and who he was talking to.

- *Know your audience.* Kerry and his inner circle decided to place great emphasis on his military record, with a parallel decision to try to focus attention on George Bush's military record (or lack thereof). This was a strategic error. There were plenty of current issues to discuss in that campaign, and I suspect that the American people were more concerned with the Iraq War and the economy than with the Vietnam War.

- *Speak the language of decisiveness.* Is John Kerry decisive? He probably is more so than was portrayed in the 2004 presidential campaign, but he needed to change his speech pattern dramatically. He needed to leave the subordinate clauses at home. Shorten his sentences—make them declarative and simple. He was caught in the communication style of senatorial debate, which could not have been more different than the world of presidential campaign communication.

Rear-view mirror analysis is always easy. But it is also instructive, and these two presidential campaigns have presented many things that we can learn about the need for authentic, clear, and simple communication.

145

CHAPTER

7

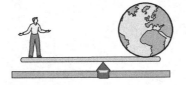

Gaining Weight, Part II: Build Credibility

Always speak to your audience as you would a group of friends in a familiar setting.

—Ronald Reagan

When you have credibility, nothing else matters. When you don't have credibility, nothing else matters.

Credibility is that elusive, intangible currency that enhances persuasion, power, and influence. It is so difficult to obtain and so easy to lose. You can't always see credibility, but you know when it is there—perhaps more importantly, you know when it isn't.

When you have credibility, your audience gives you the benefit of the doubt: The audience listens to you and stays engaged. They assume the best. They want to be on your team, work with you, follow you, and buy from you. When you don't have credibility, your audience is immediately skeptical. They stop listening to you and assume the worst. They don't trust you, and won't buy from you or willingly follow your lead.

If you have credibility, an audience that is neutral to your idea or request may still say "yes" because they trust you. There is little risk for them to support you. Conversely, if you lack credibility, a neutral audience will often say "no." Even if they do not have negative feelings about your product or company or cause, they are likely to say "no" because they have negative feelings about you. Despite all the other factors that contribute to successful persuasion, credibility makes it all possible—or impossible.

Revisiting the Leverage Metaphor

Let's take another look at the Leverage Metaphor from Chapter 2. You now have a good knowledge of your audience, allowing you to move your figurative fulcrum as close as possible to your goal of lifting your audience. You have crafted an appropriate, articulate message, which makes your figurative lever as long and strong as possible. But what else can you do to achieve additional mechanical advantage, to increase your chances of persuading your audience?

The third and final variable available to you in your attempt to lift that heavy object is the weight, or force, you can apply on your end of the lever. The final variable is you, your credibility, and the respect the audience has for you. The more credibility you have with your audience, the more figurative force you can apply to your end of the lever. Moving the fulcrum and understanding your audience is critical. Having the longest possible lever, and the correct message, is equally critical. And the final variable—your weight on the lever, your credibility—is just as critical as the other two (see Figure 7.1).

We need to find ways for you to gain weight so we can apply greater force to your end of the lever. We need to make you into a heavyweight. No one wants to be a lightweight because they can't move anything. Lightweights don't sell, lead, or attract new investors. In showing you how to move the world, I am offering you increased "weight" in a figurative sense. I am showing you how to become a heavyweight when you walk into a room.

Ultimately, we seek to have all aspects of the GAP Method in our favor. We want good Goals, a good under-

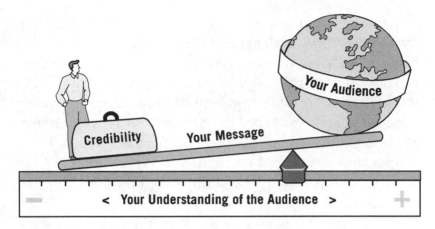

Figure 7.1 The final piece of the leverage metaphor is your credibility, the weight you bring to the table.

standing of our Audience, a good Plan. We also want all three variables of the Leverage Metaphor in our favor as well. We want to understand our audience, have a strong message, and have tons of credibility. The way you are perceived by your audience will have a significant impact on your ability to persuade them. We can follow everything we have talked about thus far in this book, but without credibility we will struggle to achieve our goals.

Credibility Given— Credibility Earned

In the most macro terms, there are two ways you are granted credibility by the people you communicate with—think of this credibility in terms of a financial investment.

Initially, your audience may make an investment in you, which gives you a small deposit of credibility. How does this happen? Your job title can earn you some credibility. Your newness in your role can also earn you some credibility. If things have not previously gone well, your arrival can spring hope—and hope can breed credibility. Your reputation may also add to the credibility deposit people make in you. Until people know you based on their own experience, they are likely to give you some credibility based on title, hope, or reputation.

Eventually, how you spend your initial credibility investment is based on your presence, your words, and your performance. Over time, credibility must be earned. Initially it can be given, but credibility that is automatically awarded is not inexhaustible. You must take that initial credibility investment and use it to grow more credibility. The credibility that you grow or that you *earn* is the credibility that will endure.

Let's illustrate the point by way of a story from my personal life. The lessons illustrated in this story can apply to everything we do—professionally and personally.

Jim, the Dad

I have a good friend, someone whom I respect greatly, who is a father of three boys in high school. I have known his family for many years, and I knew him well before he married and started a family. We'll refer to this friend as "Jim."

Jim and I don't see each other often anymore, but we do get together about once a year. Over the past few years,

I have noticed a big change in how he interacts with his boys. More important, I have seen a big change in how his boys react to Jim.

When Jim was in school, he was a bit of a hellion. He is highly successful now, but throughout his adolescent and college years Jim was known more for having fun than for high achievement. He had his brushes with authority, rigidly resisted rules, and charted his own course all the time. He is, and has always been, a free thinker. This aspect of his character has served him well, and Jim is proud of these character traits. He talks about them all the time and still enjoys spinning a good yarn about the trouble he got into in his younger years.

Now, as an adult, Jim's household is run as a tight ship. There is a clear set of rules, plenty of household chores for all the boys, and family dinner several times a week. He expects a lot of his boys and could easily be classified as a "disciplinarian." Around the house, beds are expected to be made every day, tables cleared, dishes washed, and so on. But these rules don't apply to Jim as often as they apply to everyone else. Jim is the dad, and dads don't have to do certain things in Jim's household.

In the past two years, Jim has confided in me several times that his boys don't listen to him anymore and that they have become disrespectful. The older boys have gotten into some trouble in school as well. He has tried to tighten the controls and convince his boys they are following the wrong path, but they roll their eyes, "yes" him to death, and continue their behavior unmodified. This never used to happen, according to Jim. When his boys were younger, the relationship was great, the boys

153

looked up to him, and they did as they were told. But this is no longer true.

Lessons from Jim

When I think of the Jim I knew as a son, and compare him to the Jim I know as a father, his management style could best be described as "do as I say, not as I do." And when I think about the growing tension between Jim and his boys, a few things seem clear. (Let me underscore that this passage is under no circumstances a commentary on good parenting versus bad parenting.) I believe that Jim's growing disconnect with his boys comes from a perceived double standard and, over time, a loss of his credibility. This is the aspect of this personal story that gives us a learning opportunity for our professional lives.

I've seen many other examples of the double standard in their household: children chided for an unmade bed while the parents' bed remained unmade; children punished for missing commitments yet the parent broke a promise to attend a game; and there was even a stiff punishment for missing curfew and coming home drunk even though Dad has bragged that he used to do it "all the time." As his boys have gotten older, they have become aware of different rules for different people in their household, and this is a hard thing for human beings to accept.

There are certainly differences between the family dynamic and the professional dynamic and so I readily acknowledge that I am not comparing apples directly to apples. However, the ways in which we communicate, develop credibility, and earn each other's respect do transfer from our personal lives to our professional lives and back again. Think about the teacher who reduces a grade when a paper is turned in late, but then blatantly ignores the promised date to return graded papers. Think about the store manager who holds his shift managers to different standards of accuracy when counting the cash in the register. We could design many examples along these lines.

Jim and his boys are a real-life, painful story that illustrates one of the quickest ways to erode credibility. If you regularly demonstrate that you hold the people in your life—personal or professional—to a different standard than you hold for yourself, you will have a hard time earning their respect. I am not suggesting that parents should take out the trash as often as the kids do; however, Jim was given a certain amount of respect and credibility as the father of the house that has eroded over time because he did not continually earn it.

Credibility—How to Get It

From personal lives to professional lives, there are six ways to earn credibility:

1. *Do you know what you are talking about?* One of the major themes of this book has been that your substance is far more important than your style. So we lead this section with advice consistent with that theme. The most important way to achieve credibility is simple: know your subject matter. Be an expert in your field.

Be able to answer questions. Understand your industry (or organization, competition, or market) well enough that you can discuss it creatively, strategically, and tactically. A thorough understanding of your area of expertise will put you in demand and give you a healthy head start in the quest for credibility.

2. *What is your track record of success?* There is no replacement for delivering the goods. People tend to want to do business with other people who deliver. We are more likely to follow, buy from, hire, or partner with people who have a history of success. There are many ways to define success, but, in general, if you want to develop credibility, work hard to make sure the projects you are involved in achieve their goals and reach the desired outcome.

   One of the fatal flaws I frequently see is too much focus on what is yet to come. I see too many people in the pursuit of success think 10 steps ahead and lose sight of the steps immediately in front of them. It is important to look ahead and anticipate what is coming, but keep an eye on the moment and take care of business in the present. If you want credibility, make sure the projects you are involved in today are successful. Credibility is best built over time, and the time to start is now. If you spend too much time worrying about what happens tomorrow, you'll fumble today and set yourself back in your credibility quest.

3. *Do you manage or inflate expectations?* If, in your effort to make the sale or shape opinion on a topic, you over-promise or inflate the expectations of others, you will make it hard to meet those expectations. And if you

156

continually fail to meet the expectations you create in others, your credibility will disappear rapidly.

Now, this is not an argument for lowering the bar so much that it is easy for you to step over it. Consistently setting a low bar of expectation will be quickly recognized by your audience and will also erode your credibility. It is a fine line. Be ambitious in your goal setting, and in the ways you build up the expectations of your clients or employees, but if you are overly ambitious or unrealistic, or if you set expectations so high that you will never meet them, then credibility will be elusive.

4. *Do you execute solutions or just make promises?* Our business culture has an overdeveloped sense of marketing and advertising. I say overdeveloped because, at times, we put more emphasis on the perception than the reality and style over substance. At times, we put all our effort into making promises and closing the sale, and considerably less time in delivering on the promises. Do you want some proof? Call for technical support sometime on a product you already own. See how long you wait on hold. Then call the same company and choose the option for the sales department. How long did you wait this time? Not nearly as long, I imagine— which is exactly my point.

You want to build some credibility? Make it clear to the people who work with you that time and again, you deliver what you say you will deliver. Return phone calls promptly. Get the job done, and when possible, don't pass it off to someone else in your organization. See that it gets done yourself. Execution builds credibility. The best way to prove execution is with actions, not words. It's not enough to say you will execute. You have to actually do it.

5. *Do you outperform expectations?* See Points 3 and 4 and follow a simple equation: exceed expectations through effective execution equals credibility.

6. *Do you communicate effectively?* There are many ways to connect communication and credibility, so we should break this single question down into several:

   - *Do you communicate honestly?* More often than not, we know when people are being straight and honest with us, and when they are not. If you develop the reputation of speaking honestly, people will begin to trust what you say. If, instead, you speak in half-truths, if you only tell the part of the story that is convenient for you, or if you are in any way dishonest in your communication, any hope of credibility is gone.

   - *How transparent is your process?* Do the people in your organization understand how decisions are made? Or is it a mystery? Human beings appreciate understanding how their fate is determined. They want to know how promotions, raises, and bonuses will be determined. They want to know how you reach the decisions you make. Even if people don't agree with what you decide, you can generate great credibility by explaining the way you made your decision.

   - *Do you take responsibility when things go wrong?* In a world where perception is all too often treated as king, the person who steps forward to accept responsibility eventually generates significant respect and credibility. It may hurt in the short term, but in the long run, accepting responsibility for failure (when appropriate to do so) is critical to the credibility equation.

- *Do you share credit when things go well?* One of the most effective methods for developing credibility is to spread credit around when things go well. Conversely, one of the quickest ways to erode credibility is to grab the spotlight. If you spread around the credit for success, and you truly did a good job and deserve some of the credit yourself, it will come back to you. And if you spread credit around selflessly, the credit that comes back to you also will outweigh what was available initially.

- *Can you evaluate progress objectively, including your own?* You will develop great credibility when you show your colleagues, peers, subordinates, and superiors that you can look at yourself and your team objectively. The people around you will quickly realize if you only see your world through the clichéd rose-colored glasses. But if you can demonstrate objectivity, people will trust your judgment, which builds credibility.

- *How often do you ask others what they think?* Someone once told me that the most empowering four words you can utter to any colleague or employee are: "What do you think?" There are many styles of leadership that can work, and different times require different leaders. In general, the most effective style I have seen includes a collaborative approach where the leaders make it clear to the people around them that they have a stake in the outcome. Nothing creates focus or alignment more quickly than real ownership. As Warren Buffett wrote, "No one washes a rental car." By giving the people around you a say in the outcome, they are no longer renters. They become owners.

The same is true in every persuasive opportunity. Persuasion requires credibility, and credibility requires that you show an interest in asking people for their opinion.

- *How well do you listen?* Following the previous point, asking questions is not enough. Listening to the answers also is required. One of the primary themes of this book is that you must understand your audience before you can persuade them of anything. To understand someone, you need to learn about them. To learn about them, you need to ask questions and listen to the answers. If you want people to listen to you and respect you, show them that you listen to them and respect them. Nothing adds credibility more quickly than listening to what people have to say. In a world dominated by television's talking heads and experts, actually listening to others and showing an interest in what they have to contribute has become a lost art.

- *Do you adopt a different, slick persona, or are you authentic?* Referring back to a theme from Chapter 6, we erode our credibility when people see us adopt different personas in different situations. I am not suggesting that the way we speak to our customers publicly, for example, should be the exact same way we speak to our best friends privately. But in general, people recognize authenticity and appreciate it. We realize when someone shows that they trust us by being themselves, and this develops significant credibility.

Once you develop credibility, you increase the metaphorical weight you can apply to your end of the lever, increasing your chances of persuasion and success.

Credibility: How to Keep It

You've worked hard to obtain credibility. The list in the previous section will help you build it, but once you have it, how do you keep it? Maintaining credibility is absolutely no different than obtaining it in the first place. Everything you did to gain credibility you must continue doing to maintain it. It is that simple.

The challenge and importance of credibility always remains the same. It is a never-ending battle to get it and keep it. You are given some initially, but as I said earlier in this chapter, it won't last. You need to spend that initial investment wisely. If you do so, you can significantly increase your credibility, which will increase your leverage and your powers of persuasion dramatically.

If you remember nothing else from this chapter, remember this: Credibility granted to you is fine—it exists, is important and there is some power in it—but credibility earned endures. The credibility you earn for yourself will give you the power to achieve your goals and will turn you into a heavyweight.

Generating credibility is one of the most important aspects of persuasion and will give you enormous amounts of leverage.

161

Ronald Wilson Reagan (1911–2004)

President Ronald Reagan passed away in 2004, and there have been volumes of literature written about him, his presidency, and his character. At this point, how do you say something original and interesting about him? It's hard, but the man and his legacy are compelling enough to encourage me to try. As with everything else in this book, this is a commentary on how we communicate and most definitely not a political commentary.

What I miss most about him has absolutely nothing to do with politics. He was indeed a polarizing political figure, as most presidents are. But love him or hate him, there are some things worth remembering and appreciating about President Reagan.

You knew exactly where he stood. We now live in an age of shifting politics, spin, and media double-talk. Our leaders are more polarized and nasty toward each other than ever before. They take polls, decide what is important to the electorate on that day or week, and then craft a message that hits the electorate's hot buttons.

President Reagan had firm convictions. Many years after he left office, we still know exactly what mattered to him and what he believed in. As a point of comparison, try and list the four or five most important issues for any of our past three presidents or several major party candidates. Perhaps we might all agree on one or two. But President Reagan's primary convictions were crystal clear, and whether you agreed or not, you knew what they were. Remember Dr. Martin Luther King, Jr.'s famous quotation on leadership: "A genuine leader is not a searcher for consensus but a molder of consensus."

Not only did President Reagan have convictions, he communicated them brilliantly. His style had all the attributes of good communication—it was crisp, clear, and consistent. And for those who agreed with his politics, his communication was convincing and compelling.

President Reagan's communication skills helped him instill a sense of confidence and international pride for Americans. When Reagan took office in January 1981, national confidence was near an all-time low. The Russians were on the advance; we had been powerless to free our hostages in Iran; gas prices, interest rates, inflation, and unemployment were frighteningly high; and Watergate was still fresh in our national consciousness. President Carter had it right when he called it a "crisis of confidence." Yet eight years later, the entire national mood had shifted, and

(continued)

there is no denying that President Reagan had a great deal to do with that confidence boost.

What's more, even his most heated political opponents liked him personally. By all accounts, this was a decent and kind man. They may have hated his politics, but they never hated the man. How many other presidents can we say that about? How about the current one? How about the past one?

Finally, President Reagan brought dignity to the office. His political legacy can be debated, depending on your disposition, but his personal legacy is beyond reproach—no personal scandals.

He had conviction, clarity, decency, and dignity. He provided timely and timeless lessons in communication, leadership, and, most important, character. The legacy of Reagan, the politician, is still being debated and written, but the legacy of Reagan, the man, is already etched in stone.

8

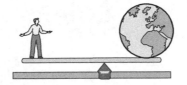

If You Remember Nothing Else, Remember These Things

Give me a lever long enough and a fulcrum on which to place it, and I shall move the world.

—Archimedes

When I step back and think about our professional culture, I continually have the same realization. *We make things harder for ourselves than they have to be.* How? Repeating the point made in Chapter 1, our communication is not as clear or as effective as it could be. We waste enormous amounts of time constructing (or watching) poorly-organized presentations, giving (or listening to) directionless and passion-free speeches, participating in meetings that lack action steps or conducting meetings with the wrong message. When we don't communicate in the correct way, we don't make the sale, we leave opportunity on the table and, yes, we make things harder than they should be—or could be.

We have relied on the spoken word and language to communicate with each other since the beginning of time. Yet as our professions become endlessly more complicated, with more demands and requirements placed upon on us than ever before, many individuals and organizations have lost sight of the fundamentals. While we are flooded with the latest "hot" products, services or ideas every day, few people spend time and resources on a skill that is not new— the skill of articulate expression.

This brings us to one of the basic principles of this book. *Because* life is so much more complicated, focusing on simple articulate and persuasive communication will offer you a competitive advantage.

This book is not about the hot new idea or product. This book is about giving you simple, but critical, ways to think about the common act of communication and to help you do it an uncommon way. This book is about helping you harness the power of language so you can persuade others to see what you see, or to do what you would like them to do.

The Search for Simplicity— Metaphor and Method

The two primary ideas presented in this book are designed to get us back to the basics of communication: a *metaphor* to help you think about persuasive communication and the critical aspects of it and a *method* to help you prepare your plan to persuade your audience. The Leverage Metaphor and the GAP Method are designed to simplify the things you have to remember. They are designed to give you simple and effective ways to increase your powers of persuasion. Together, the Leverage Metaphor and the GAP Method comprise the *Move the World* System. Although some of the individual ideas within the System are not new, the System itself is new—and it is the System as a whole that will increase your power to persuade.

Let's look back and quickly review the essential elements of both the Metaphor and the Method (see Figure 8.1).

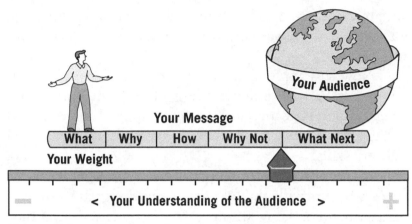

Figure 8.1   The formula for persuasive success? Know your audience, construct a strong message, and have plenty of personal credibility.

Remember the Metaphor

The first important concept in this book, the *Leverage Metaphor*, provides a way to *think* about how to communicate.

A lever and a fulcrum will help you lift something that greatly outweighs you, and that you would not otherwise be able to lift on your own. The Leverage Metaphor serves to remind you about the critical communication variables that will help you lift your audience and persuade them to do the things you want them to do.

The concept is simple, but the potential power is significant. There are three ways you can increase your ability to achieve your goals. First, you can move the fulcrum closer to the object you want to lift. Second, you can find or create a longer lever. And, third, you can apply more force on your end of the lever. When any one of these variables is in your favor, your power increases. But when all three of these variables are in your favor, your power multiplies.

Now let's apply it to communication: Your fulcrum is equivalent to your understanding of your audience; your lever is your message; and the force applied on your end of the lever is you—your reputation, credibility, and verbal delivery skills.

When you attempt to persuade your audience, your success begins with the fulcrum. Everything else becomes easier when you know who your audience is and what they care about. When you move your fulcrum closer to your audience, when you understand who they are and what they believe, it becomes possible to design the most powerful and persuasive message for them. Moving the fulcrum toward the audience allows for a longer, stronger, and more appropriate lever. When you can demonstrate to your audience that you understand them and their issues, and you can show that you have designed a message that anticipated their concerns, you automatically have more credibility as a speaker. You automatically increase your force on your end of the lever.

There are many applications to having increased leverage:

- In a political sense, communication leverage is the ability to exert greater influence on your electorate and persuade them to make their voting decision based on variables that favor you. If you have the better economic plan and you can make the economy the most important variable in the election, you will have gone

170

a long way toward winning the race. You will have persuaded your audience—voters—to choose based on something that favors you.

- In a managerial sense, communication leverage is the ability to get more out of the resources around you by streamlining your structure, motivating your team, or securing the extra resources your people need to succeed.

- In a fund-raising sense, communication leverage is the ability to share your vision with your audience in a way that makes them want to support you and your organization.

- A sales environment is much like the political environment. You need to convince your market to make their buying decision based on the variables that favor you and your product, service, or organization. A buying decision is very similar to a vote. Your communication leverage will help you influence that buying decision.

- And in a leadership environment, your communication leverage will allow you to align your team around the goals you set, convincing your people to adopt the strategy and work together.

In all these examples, and in many others, a thorough understanding of the audience, the correct message, and plenty of credibility as a speaker will make your life easier and will enhance your leverage as a professional. The Leverage Metaphor helps us understand and remember the areas that will help us increase our power.

171

Remember the Method

The second important concept in this book, the *GAP Method*, provides a simple but powerful way to *prepare* to communicate—what to say and how to say it. You need to have Goals, understand your Audience, and have a Plan to persuade. These are the fundamental pillars of persuasion.

Although the truly persuasive person is rare, the Building Blocks of Persuasion are simple to grasp and are easily understood by all of us. So why, if we all already know the fundamental pillars of persuasion, do so many of us struggle with how to persuade? I hope my simple system will make it easier for you to prepare for communication in your otherwise busy life.

We devoted a large percentage of this book to breaking down the elements of the GAP Method. Now, every time you enter into a communication opportunity, I hope you will think about your goals. What do you want people to think about or do when you are done? I encourage you to spend time prior to your communication opportunity thinking about your audience. Who are they? What do they care about? What will cause them to say "yes"? What will cause them to say "no"? Finally, I encourage you to think about the relationship between your goal (your end point) and the audiences' current perception (the starting point) to create a plan and message that will help you connect those two points. Ask yourself these questions: What do I have to do to change minds? What do I have to say or demonstrate to persuade? How do I guide these people with my words and cause them to think or act differently?

This is the essence of persuasion—changing people's

thinking from where it is today, to where you want it to be tomorrow. Successful persuasion is not easy, and at times it will not be possible. Certain minds cannot and will not be changed: The hard-line Democrat won't vote Republican or vice versa. The Yankee fan will not cheer for the Red Sox. But the GAP Method is your road map for increasing your chances for success—think about your Goals, Audience, and Plan. If you routinely prepare in the proper way, you will change minds and achieve your goals more often than not.

Critical Themes to Remember

I hope you take away the following critical themes from this book:

- *Focus on the audience.* Both the Metaphor and the Method possess the same core—an understanding of your audience. Knowing as much as possible about the person or people you are attempting to persuade is essential to achieve your goals.

- *Focus on earning credibility.* Just as important, however, is your ability to develop credibility as a person and a professional. When people believe you (and *in* you), trust you, respect you, and like you, everything becomes easier. When you have credibility, nothing else matters. When you don't have credibility, nothing else matters. And this focus on audience and credibility are woven tightly together. The more you understand your audience, the more credibility you will be able to earn.

- *Be clear in what you say.* Subtlety can work in your favor in certain, specific instances, but the vast majority of the time, your professional communication will be enhanced by the ability to tell people in a concise way what your point is. Don't make your audience work hard to understand you. If you do, most of them will choose not to put in the time. If you want to be effective, be clear. Think through what you want to say and use as few words as possible.

- *Clearly demonstrate value to your audience.* Human beings almost always require some sort of benefit before they can be persuaded. One of the quickest ways to reach a successful outcome and persuade your audience is to clearly demonstrate "what's in it for them."

- *Don't distract your audience.* This is the one simple rule for effective delivery. It is your litmus test. Do you do anything that is distracting or otherwise annoying to the people listening to you? If the answer is "no," then you are already in the ballpark of effectiveness. If the answer is "yes," then look to tone down that habit, eliminate that verbal pause ("um"), or reduce that verbal tick.

- *Be authentic.* If you take a class or read a book that tells you that you will need to fundamentally change who you are when you stand up to speak, quit the class or put the book down. It's not true. I'm not suggesting that a few modifications in your voice or style won't be useful. Some coaching and some modifications may be necessary. But those modifications should be made within the range of your authentic self. If you speak with a colloquial and conversational style, and that style is appropriate for your audience, the last thing you should do is adopt a formal way of speaking. Just be yourself and you'll show the audience that you have confidence and that you trust them. They'll be more likely to trust you.

Final Thoughts

My final thoughts to you concern the importance of persuasion and the need for a focus on articulate expression and powerful, persuasive speech.

When you have the power of persuasion, your ideas are heard. Your strategies are adopted. You can align your team and manage your project to successful completion. Being persuasive automatically makes you a better leader.

When you have the power of persuasion, you are able to sell your products more effectively. You are able to raise more capital. You are able to represent yourself and your organization well. You are able to persuade your clients and prospects to view your products or services the way you want them to be viewed.

When you have the power of persuasion, you are able to help others and take everyone on your team to a higher level. People want to be on your team. You are in demand. Interviews become easier. When you have the power of persuasion, you are able to make your case when negotiating a raise.

I could go on and on. The simple reality is this: The person who has the ability to persuasively and articulately communicate their message has a significant competitive advantage.

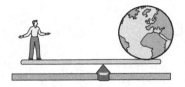

An Invitation to Change Your Life, Part II

Many athletes have the will to win. But only a few have the will to prepare to win.

—John Wooden

began this book with an invitation to you, the reader. In the Preface, I invited you to consider that the simple but potent concepts and tools contained in this book could have the power to change your life. Since you've gotten this far, I should pause and say "thank you" for accepting my invitation and for reading *Move the World*.

I would like to return to that initial invitation and expand on it. You have taken the first critical step of considering some new ideas and have committed the time to read this book. You are well on your way to acquiring the power of persuasion, but your work is far from done.

I teach communication for a living. I run training classes, coach people in small groups or as individuals, and speak at conferences on the topic of communication. Communication is my life's work. I take my work seriously, and few things in life give me greater satisfaction than helping a client achieve their goals through more effective communication. However, as much as I want to help my clients, I can honestly state that not everyone who works with me and The Latimer Group achieves their goals. Not everyone I work with becomes a world-class communicator. Not everyone who reads this book will automatically and dramatically improve. And not everyone will develop the ability to *move the world*.

Because books, classes, and coaching are only tools, they cannot offer magical solutions. Some classes and some books promise the consumer quick fixes and shortcuts to success. Such promises are unrealistic and insulting to your intelligence. No book or class can or should offer guaranteed success. Think again about the discussion of tools versus skills from Chapter 1. If you own a hammer, it can help you build a house. But simply owning a hammer does not make you a qualified carpenter. Reading a book on carpentry will not automatically qualify you to build a house. To become a qualified carpenter and to learn how to construct a house, you must practice and develop skills. This is true of your communication skills, too.

You probably already own the tools of communication, or at least some of them, and reading *Move the World* or taking classes are important next steps. But owning the tools, reading the book, or taking a class will not be enough. To dramatically improve your skills, you must apply what you have learned.

I began this book by inviting you to read it and consider new ideas. Now I am inviting you to make an honest attempt to improve your communication skills through the *Move the World* System. Before your next communication opportunity, consider your leverage. Consider your Goals, attempt to understand your Audience, and create a thoughtful Plan to persuade. I cannot, and will not, guarantee you success, but I promise that applying this System will improve your chances to persuade.

The step after the initial application of a new principle is practice. As with any new skill, continual practice is required to progress to competency and eventually to expertise. The famous golfer Ben Hogan once said, "Golf is a game of luck. The more I practice, the luckier I get." This book is a road map, giving you the steps to take so that you can improve and become a powerful and persuasive communicator. Your power from here will depend on what you do with the knowledge, tools, and frameworks contained herein. If you put the concepts you have learned into regular practice, you will enjoy tangible benefits. This book is valuable, but it is no magic bullet. I don't believe magic bullets exist, at least when it comes to developing important business skills like persuasive communication.

The abilities to persuade and communicate effectively are among the most important skills you can have at your disposal. People who can speak well—stand up and speak coherently in front of a group, take control of a meeting with an articulate point, or say the right thing in an interview or on a sales call—are rare. The people who can speak well stand out, are in demand, and tend to succeed. This ability to articulate and persuade will serve us well in almost every aspect of our lives. When we are in the presence of those who can make a point articulately and persuasively in a room of 5 or 500, we are impressed. We remember their *names*, their *presence*, and their *power*. I want people to remember *your* name, *your* presence, and *your* power. I want you to develop the power of persuasion.

Acquiring this skill will help you reach your goals, both professionally and personally. Taking classes or reading books like *Move the World* are great steps toward acquiring what you need to succeed, but there are other steps still in front of you. Will you take the next steps? Will you apply what you have learned and practice the craft of persuasive communication?

As you consider these last few questions, I close and ask you to think about the words of John Wooden that appears at the beginning of this postscript: "Many athletes have the will to win. But only a select few have the will to *prepare* to win." Do you?

Good luck!